The Century of the Sun

The Century of

THE FIRST HUNDRED YEARS

OF SUN LIFE

ASSURANCE COMPANY OF CANADA

the Sun

Joseph Schull

1971

MACMILLAN OF CANADA TORONTO

Other Books by Joseph Schull

The Legend of Ghost Lagoon
I, Jones, Soldier
The Far Distant Ships
The Salt Water Men
The Battle for the Rock
Ships of the Great Days
100 Years of Banking in Canada
Laurier, the First Canadian
The Jinker
The Nation Makers

Printed in Canada
for The Macmillan Company of Canada Limited
70 Bond Street, Toronto 2

Foreword

One hundred years, measured against the centuries of recorded history, is but a short span of time. Yet in terms of the lives of men and women – the people who create and maintain enduring institutions – a century is a sufficiently lengthy period to justify the writing of an historical record. The object of this book is therefore to record at this important anniversary, while sources of information are readily available, the opportunities that were seized and the problems that were encountered in the building of a great Canadian company.

Our desire was to have a brief, readable book available primarily for members of the Company and its friends. This Mr. Joseph Schull has accomplished with great understanding and skill. The limitation of brevity has unfortunately somewhat restricted the author's scope; there is much more of interest he could have written about and many more people whose names and deeds both he, and we, would have wished to see included.

It is our hope that readers will enjoy this account of the first hundred years and join us in our enthusiasm for the next 'Century of the Sun'.

Alistair M. Campbell

Acknowledgments

In the preparation of the first seven chapters of this book I have been much assisted by an early history of Sun Life, *The President's Book,* written by George H. Harris and published in 1928. Throughout the whole work I have had complete access to all information desired and, except where obvious errors of fact had to be corrected, I have been left free to interpret it in my own way. I have had at my disposal all the resources of the fine Historical Records Department maintained by Sun Life. In addition to this, senior officials of the company, some retired and many active in management, have been generous with their time and patient in explanation of the various aspects of an intricate and fascinating business.

I should like to thank all these men, and in particular A. R. Hasley, Vice-President, Special Duties, who made all arrangements for the work, made all records available, and was unfailingly generous in providing assistance, encouragement, and advice. I am also particularly grateful to J. Leslie Harries, Manager, Historical Records, for Sun Life, who was a constant collaborator in the work of maintaining accuracy, a mine of information, and a source of valuable suggestions as to new avenues of research. Finally, I should like to acknowledge the help of Miss Phyllis Taylor and Miss Ruth Rowe, who were responsible for the many typings and retypings necessary in the preparation of the manuscript.

Joseph Schull

Contents

Appendix

Illustrations

The Century of the Sun

1

The Founders and the Founding

MATHEW GAULT

Mathew Hamilton Gault, in the Montreal business community of 1865, was a man of considerable stature who seemed likely to rise further. Then forty-three, he had spent twenty-two years in Canada and had not found all of them easy. His father, a prosperous merchant and shipowner in Northern Ireland, had been forced to emigrate in 1842 by a series of marine disasters that wrecked both his fortune and his health. Mathew at twenty-one had found himself in Montreal, the eldest of seven children, with a dying father and a seriously ailing mother. At twenty-two, with his father dead and his mother still an invalid, he had become the head of the family.

He was troubled, as he would be all his life, by the effects of a spinal injury suffered in a fall from a horse at the age of fifteen. Much of his slender capital disappeared in the failure of a bank, and the subsequent purchase of a farm was no more profitable. For five or six years after that it was a matter of constant struggle simply to educate the younger children and keep his head above water. Then, in 1851, the change came. An alert and determined young man, tall and notably handsome despite his injury, he managed to secure the agency for the British America Assurance Company of Toronto, which transacted a general business, and also for The Mutual Life Insurance Company of New York. Mutual of New York, though only eight years old, was making giant strides in the United States and Gault kept pace in Canada. By 1865, in his office at 77 Great St. James Street, he was not only conducting a sizeable insurance business but was also manager of the Montreal branch of Toronto's Royal Canadian Bank. None of these interests, in the freewheeling business world of the 1860s, prevented him from adding others, and the younger sons of the family were well on their way too. Andrew Frederick and Robert Leslie, the next brothers in line, had become partners in a large wholesale dry goods firm that was soon to acquire textile mills and earn for Andrew Frederick the title, 'Cotton King of Canada'. Behind all the brothers lay a record of confident progress, and in Mathew particularly there was a restless spark of leadership that gave promise of bigger things.

THE CHANGING COUNTRY

The times themselves were restless, and full of confusing portents for the man who looked ahead. In the United States the terrible Civil War was drawing to a close, but the many incidents with Great Britain had left the Union surly and hostile towards the British American colonies. In the colonies themselves, after years of political turmoil, Upper and Lower Canada had joined with the Maritime provinces in the plan of Confederation. But the plan was a plan still, and there was no assurance of success. Within three months of the first conference in Charlottetown, and two months of the greater Quebec Conference, one could sense the rising backwash. Mathew Gault had only to walk the streets or read his newspaper to feel the strength of the forces opposed to union.

For ten years the Reciprocity Treaty with the United States had eliminated most tariffs and swelled trade enormously. Montreal had boomed on that prosperity and was booming still. The decade that had spanned the Canadas with the Grand Trunk Railway had widened the city's streets, pushed out its suburbs, sent up magnificent buildings. In the past year alone there had been more than

Mathew Hamilton Gault, founder of the Company and later Managing Director.

Thomas Workman, M.P., first President
of the Company, 1871-89.

St. Lawrence Hall hotel on St. James Street,
the location of the Sun's first office.

Barron Block on St. James Street, the Sun's Head Office from late 1871 until 1891.

Early coloured poster in use about 1885.

a thousand constructions of every sort. The great Victoria Bridge arched over the St. Lawrence, just five years old, and the eighth wonder of the world. Along the stone wharves of the waterfront there was a rich bustle of commerce, the new horse-car lines travelled the pleasant, paved expanses of Great St. James and Notre Dame streets, and the carriages of the well-to-do climbed from the centre of the city towards a thickening cluster of mansions along the lower slopes of Mount Royal. Yet much of this was threatened now by dislocation and change. The Reciprocity Treaty was due to expire, and would certainly not be renewed. There was the prospect of dwindling trade, rising tariffs, of depression after the boom in the old, familiar pattern. At the same time, on the other hand, there was the prospect born in Charlottetown of the new nation linked by rail with the Atlantic and one day with the Pacific. To the believer in Confederation it opened an enormous future, and Gault was one of the believers.

THE SCOPE FOR LIFE INSURANCE

He was also a pioneer who was ready for a new venture. After fourteen years with Mutual Life of New York, he was convinced of the value of his product and of the scope of his opportunity. Almost the first in its field in the United States, Mutual had grown enormously by convincing thousands of Americans that they needed life insurance. Canadians had equal need and Gault intended to supply it, by means of a native company.

He had begun work on his project early in 1864. It was proof of his quality and of the regard in which he was held that he could gather about him, for what must have been a series of long discussions, some of the keenest minds and most ambitious spirits of commercial Montreal. George Stephen, the future Lord Mount Stephen of the Canadian Pacific Railway, stands out from among them today, but Alexander Walker Ogilvie, James Hutton, James Ferrier the younger, Henry Mulholland, and half a dozen others were all household names in the mercantile world of the time. They were big men in the produce and milling business, in hardware, dry goods, and textiles, and in transportation, banking, and finance.

Their offices, shops, and warehouses lay for the most part within an easy walk of each other along Great St. James or Notre Dame or the smaller streets that linked them, and they had grown with the city's growth. They were a close-knit group with wide experience and interests, but the subject of Gault's proposal was comparatively new to them all.

They were familiar enough from their own experience with the general business of protection against fire and marine disaster. Life insurance, however, which was Gault's principal concern, was another matter entirely. Its roots went back deep into the Middle Ages, but the chances of mortality at that time had attracted mainly the speculator. For almost two hundred years, from the sixteenth century onward, Europe had been familiar with the unsavoury practice of gambling on the life expectancy of public men, some of them ailing, some of them likely prospects for assassination. By 1774, however, when that form of profit and excitement was suppressed by law, the real function of insurance had begun to emerge.

The first 'Bills of Mortality', compiled in the seventeenth century, had become reasonably accurate tables by the middle of the eighteenth. They were still further refined, as their use became apparent, by a study of the vital statistics of English towns. The 'Northampton Table' appeared in 1771, the 'Carlisle Table' in 1815, and these were followed a little later by mortality tables based on the census statistics of all England. Meanwhile, as existing insurance companies compiled their own experience, the first actuarial tables began to appear.

The fact had been grasped that, while 'men do not die in exact proportions', there is an average duration to life and a calculable cost for insurance. The level annual premium, which was the genesis of modern life insurance, had been devised for the distribution of the cost of the risk. It became possible to graduate premiums according to age, to assess the total risk on a whole life, and to divide the cost of protection into equal annual payments. Each payment, as it was made, became part of a company's reserve against the liability assumed. Yet it became also a part of a general fund which could be invested to earn interest, helping in itself to build the required reserve and decreasing the cost to the insured.

On this principle of uniform level premiums, supporting a life contract and pooled for joint investment, life insurance had grown.

A few devoted men, perplexed by the problems of the poor, had seen in it the answer to many needs. They had evolved the plans that grew to the modern policy, and broadened the statistical basis that underlay the plans. From a heartless gamble based on the lives of others, life insurance had become a personal shield and safeguard, the one means by which a man with a tithe of his earnings could protect his family while he lived and bring them certain benefit when he died.

Nevertheless, the remains of prejudice endured. In a new country like Canada few thought of life insurance and to some of those who did it seemed 'not in human nature to have money depending on the existence of an inmate of your home without entertaining feelings which the good man would tremble to analyse and even the bad man would fear to avow'. In the whole of British North America, in 1865, there was less than $15 million of life insurance in force, and three-quarters of that was with British or American companies. The Canada Life Assurance Company, founded at Hamilton in 1847 and still, after eighteen years, struggling against public apathy and suspicion of life insurance, was the only native company that had managed to gain a foothold.

Against this Gault could point to the success of Mutual of New York in the United States. He could point to Great Britain where, through 150 years, life insurance had grown and established itself, not as an instrument of greed, but as an expression of love and care. It was a business soundly based on a real human necessity, the need to provide for one's own. It was scientific in practice, and it was profitable in operation. Its tables of life expectancy and the premium rates based on them had been two hundred years in developing and were almost wholly reliable. British companies had found that they could operate safely and conservatively, providing full protection for their policyholders, with a return of 3 per cent on their invested funds. That was only half of the current return on first-class securities in Canada. A Canadian company, with a wide margin of safety, could charge lower premiums and return a profit to its shareholders. Yet at the present moment there was only one such company in existence, while the agencies of British and American companies collected well over $1 million annually in premiums. Gault proposed to keep that money, or at least some of it, at home. There was room for another company here in Canada.

CHARTERS AND ORGANIZATION

By midsummer he had convinced his listeners and by August 10, 1864, a petition drawn up by himself, George Stephen, and most of the men who met with them had been prepared for presentation to the parliament of the Canadas. There was a wait of seven months, however, before the first milestone was passed. It was not until March 18, 1865, that the petition received its assent. An act passed on that day authorized the incorporation of The Sun Insurance Company of Montreal 'to enable parties owners of or interested in property to insure the same against loss by fire, and also to carry on the business of marine and inland navigation assurance, and life assurance generally'.

Less than a week before, the same parliament of the Canadas had approved the resolution that would lead to Confederation. The new era opening before the country might have seemed an auspicious time for the rising of the new Sun. Actually, however, conditions proved very different. There were to be two stormy years before the Dominion of Canada was proclaimed, and the turmoil did not end with July 1, 1867. There was the problem of Nova Scotia, resentful and hostile still within the union. There was the problem of the North West Territories, where the taking over of the lands of the Hudson's Bay Company brought revolt at the Red River. From the United States came the threat of Fenian invaders, and the Reciprocity Treaty was duly denounced, bringing dislocation of trade. Banks failed, businessmen went bankrupt, and for a time the new nation seemed to stumble in doubt and confusion. The charter for the new company remained dormant in Gault's files.

Yet, by the opening of 1870, conditions were changing again. With all its besetting troubles, the Dominion was on the move. The Intercolonial Railway had been begun and there were already negotiations for the other railway to the Pacific. There was a promise of new provinces, and relations between the old were beginning to improve. A mass of legislation had dealt with commerce, and one act in particular was of special interest to Gault. Turning its attention to life insurance, the first parliament had stipulated for the protection of policyholders that any company transacting business in Canada must deposit $50,000 with the Dominion government.

To Mutual Life of New York, the company for which Gault was

agent, the act had posed a serious question of policy. As a mutual company it was entirely owned by its policyholders, who were mainly in the United States. To make the required deposit in another country, even though the amount was comparatively insignificant, would be to give foreign policyholders a preferred lien on its assets. The company chose instead to withdraw from Canada.

It would return in later years, but for the present the move was important. Gault had resisted it, and was even said to have offered to put up the money himself. Refused in this, he was left without a life insurance agency but with an opportunity whose scope was suddenly enlarged. In such a situation, and with general conditions in the country beginning to improve, his thoughts turned to the five-year-old charter. Discussions began again with some of his former associates, this time in St. Lawrence Hall at 131 St. James Street, where he had taken a new office.

The first outcome of these discussions was a second petition to Parliament, which was approved by an act of May 12, 1870. The amended charter, however, under the Dominion's new insurance law, required the division of the company into two branches, each separately capitalized, if it were to operate both a general business and a life and accident business. While this seems to have been accepted, and provisional directors were appointed, there must have been afterthoughts about the double requirement of capital. The first prospectus for the company, submitted to the provisional directors on October 5, 1870, was discussed and disapproved. An amended prospectus, approved on October 12, had narrowed the field proposed for operations. It informed the public that The Sun Insurance Company of Montreal had been authorized by Parliament to transact 'a general Life Insurance business'. The capital of the company was to be $1 million and subscriptions were solicited to the amount of $500,000, of which 'one-half the amount has already been taken by several of our leading citizens'. When the remaining shares were allotted there would be a 10-per-cent call and the company would commence business.

After four months the stock books were still open and $15,000 remained to be raised. But it seemed near enough. On February 9, 1871, Gault informed the provisional board of directors that $485,000 had been subscribed, and the 10-per-cent call went out. It was to be paid by February 20, and subscribers were invited to meet on February 27.

This meeting, the first meeting of the company's shareholders, was held as usual in Gault's office. There were twenty-one men present, and to these Gault announced that the statutory deposit of $50,000 had been placed with the Receiver General. The next business, the election of permanent directors, was found to be invalidated later by an 'informality' in arrangements, and it was at a second meeting on March 20 that the board of the company took shape. The name of Mathew Gault did not appear, as the post of Managing Director was reserved for him and was to be made by appointment of the board. The men chosen as the first directors of the company were Thomas Workman, John Rankin, Charles Alexander, James Hutton, Andrew Frederick Gault, T. James Claxton, Alexander Buntin, Henry Mulholland, and Charles J. Coursol. These men, at the first directors' meeting three days later, elected Thomas Workman as President and offered the nomination as Vice-President to Andrew Frederick Gault. When he declined, T. James Claxton accepted the office, and the appointment as Managing Director went to Mathew H. Gault.

It was still necessary, before the commencement of business, to adjust the company's charter to the scope of its operation. There had also been discussion of the name, and Gault, very conscious of the success of Mutual of New York, was strongly inclined to the use of the word 'mutual'. For a stock company it was a misnomer, and would be corrected years later. At the moment, however, the directors agreed with Gault, and the Dominion parliament assented to another revised petition. An act passed on April 14, 1871, incorporated The Sun Mutual Life Insurance Company of Montreal, with powers restricted to life and accident insurance.

Another month was occupied with the bustle of organization and the appointment of company officers. Thomas Craig, a brother-in-law of Gault who had acted as provisional Secretary, was persuaded to remain in the post. For the medical staff, William Fraser, M.D., was appointed consulting physician, George Wilkins, M.D.,M.R.C.S.Eng., medical examiner, English, and Hector Peltier, M.D., medical examiner, French. In the Honourable J. J. C. Abbott, Q.C., a distinguished shareholder who became legal adviser, the company acquired the services of a future prime minister. Meanwhile by-laws were drafted, application forms and the design for a seal approved, and the Managing Director was authorized 'to prepare a form of policy and get it printed'.

THE FIRST DIRECTORS

As the last details were arranged and the time for commencement approached, the new corporate body began to take on life and character. The directors were gathered often in Gault's office around the desk that has become a company heirloom. George Stephen was not among them; his interests were veering away towards banking and railways. Alexander Walker Ogilvie, another of the men who had signed the first petition, would not be a member of the board for two years. James Hutton and Henry Mulholland, the two original signers who, with Mathew Hamilton Gault, had become directors, were importers and merchants in hardware and cutlery, prominent in the business life of the community. Charles J. Coursol was mayor of Montreal, a popular and wealthy lawyer. As rich as any among them was Alexander Buntin, with the hands of an old sailor and his paper mills at Valleyfield, proud of his wealth in a downright Scots way. Compared to Croesus once, he had made a notable reply. 'Weel, I dinna ken wha Croesus is, but for ivery dollar he'll pit doon I'll pit doon anither.' Andrew Frederick Gault, John Rankin, Charles Alexander, and T. James Claxton were equally men of means; and presiding now in the chair, as he would for eighteen years, was the tall, dignified figure of Thomas Workman. Hardware merchant, banker, and member of the Dominion parliament, he had played a distinguished part for many years in the growth of the city and the province. So had T. James Claxton, who imported ideas with dry goods and had brought the Y.M.C.A. to Montreal. Taken in all, they presented a picture of solid Victorian affluence, and rather more than that. They were a good cross-section of the talents that had made the country, and a man who believed in the country could believe in them.

2

First Steps

THE SUN RISES

On May 11, 1871, the Board of Directors met for the first time to consider prospective business. To the young company from a friendly-disposed elder, The Canada Life Assurance Company, came an application for a reinsurance of $5,000 on the life of one John Lamb of Toronto. On the second of the two forms submitted by the Managing Director, John S. Warnock of Montreal applied for a life policy in the amount of $2,000. It was considered by the directors that the family history of Mr. Lamb was unsatisfactory and the application was declined. The application of Mr. Warnock was 'referred to the medical examiner' and the day's work was over.

The meeting of May 18 was more productive. By that time Mathew H. Gault and T. James Claxton had both passed through the hands of Dr. Wilkins, the medical examiner, and so had three other applicants who were not members of the board. All applications were approved, for a total of $32,500, and it was decided that the issue date of the policies should be May 1. To Mathew H. Gault, as the first of his five policies, each for $2,000, went Policy No. 1.

From that date the weekly directors' meetings became an established routine. They were to go on for forty-four years, supplemented very often by special meetings, and for eleven of those years the hard-working members of the board would pass individually on each application submitted. The locale of the gatherings, however, was soon changed.

Gault, in taking on the management of the Sun, had retained his general business and now found that his rapidly expanding interests required more office space. From 131 St. James Street he moved west to 164 St. James Street as the handsome new Barron Block came to completion, dominating the business section with its four tall storeys and its rows of high-arched windows. Here, in a section of Gault's quarters on the ground floor, desks were reserved for Thomas Craig, the Secretary, and W. J. T. Louson, the bookkeeper, who comprised the staff of the Sun. At the rear of the general office, divided off by a partition, was a section that served as a board room, and it was here the directors met on Thursday of each week. It was here also, on Thursday, March 7, 1872, that the shareholders came to join them for the first annual meeting.

There was a good deal to report. From the time of the board's election to the close of the year, the directors had met no fewer than fifty-four times. They had made considerable progress in the work of organization. Gault, as Chief Agent, had now a second agent in Montreal. The first outside agent, William Hedley of Halifax, had been appointed on May 18. Since then the Managing Director, travelling through Quebec and 'the west', had made arrangements for representation in Quebec City, Sorel, St-Jérôme, Toronto, Hamilton, Woodstock, Guelph, and Dundas. The agreements with agents varied and some were rather sketchy, but they had produced a trickle of business by the early fall months. For the year, a total of 158 applications had been received and 148 accepted. Insurance had been granted to the amount of $404,000 and the total of premiums stood at $13,975.02. The company had made its first mortgage loan of $5,000 on September 7, and had acquired in the course of the year several shares of stock in The Canadian Bank of Commerce, the Bank of Montreal, and the Merchants Bank of Canada. There had been no death claims, and all expenses of management had been more than met by interest on capital and investments and by the rise in the value of securities. Though they declared no dividend and accepted no remuneration, the directors were modestly proud of their work to date. In a year of difficult beginnings the company had paid its way.

PROGRESS AND THE POLICY

For two more years they were able to greet the shareholders with the same restrained optimism. If it was hard to claim great progress it was easy to point to the obstacles overcome. The country was raw and new outside its cities, and the cities themselves were small. The 'west' that Gault spoke of ended with the western railhead at Georgian Bay. The hope of the C.P.R. was dying with the Pacific Scandal, and would not be resurrected for seven years. The Intercolonial to the east was only beginning to be built. Travel was difficult, communications were slow, and, particularly in the rural areas, the old, enduring prejudices waited to discourage the agent of life insurance. For thousands of unsold prospects it was still unnatural 'to have a pecuniary interest in the death of anyone'.

The agent of the Sun went out offering standard life and endowment plans that differed little from those of his competitors, and the rates he carried on his printed slips had been built up by averaging the rates charged by the most conservative British and American companies. The insurance policy itself, like all policies of the day, had a grim-visaged text that forbade as much as it offered. The prospective policyholder, if he wished his heirs to benefit by his decease, was forbidden to die by suicide, duelling, or the hands of justice. His policy was voided if he travelled the seas in any but first-class steamers or sailing vessels on regularly scheduled voyages between Europe and North America. He could enter no military or naval service, and in the hot months of the year he was forbidden the unhealthy 'south' of the United States. He could not reside between May and October below the latitude 36 degrees 33 minutes north, approximately the line of the old Missouri Compromise established in 1820 against the advance of slavery. Moreover, should he comply with all conditions and still exceed by one day the thirty days from due date allowed for the payment of premium, his policy lapsed with forfeiture of all payments.

Gault faced his difficulties with much energy and intelligence, and he had the support of the directors. It seems to have been recognized from the beginning that the improvement of the policy itself was a major object. In 1872 the first rates manual was issued, and although this was still based on an averaging of the rates of competitors there were certain notable advances. For the education of the public the manual carried 'Ten Reasons Why You Should

Insure Your Life in The Sun Mutual Life Insurance Company of Montreal'. It supported the reasons with the first cautious departure from old restrictions. Policyholders were now permitted to serve in militia or volunteer forces without extra charge. Some of the conditions of travel were slightly relaxed. More important, it was now made possible for the policyholder who discontinued after at least two annual premiums to receive the equivalent amount in paid-up insurance. With this significant first step, the Sun felt justified in claiming that its 'non-forfeitable' policy was 'more favourable than the policy of any other company doing business in Canada'.

By the end of 1872 agents had been acquired at Ottawa, Pembroke, Smiths Falls, Belleville, and Port Hope. Quebec was reasonably productive and from Halifax the work of canvassing was extending through the Maritime provinces. Agency arrangements were still loose and supervision was difficult, but business was coming in. It seemed enough to the directors to justify a shareholders' first dividend of 6 per cent, which was considerably less than the interest earned on their capital.

April of 1873 brought the company's first death claim, and by the end of the year the total of claims reported stood at $6,000. The figure was much below the reserves set up, and justified, in the directors' opinion, the careful selection of risks and the cautious policy of the company. Seasoned now by almost three years in business, they referred with somewhat premature enthusiasm to the 'past success, present standing, reputation and prospects' which 'furnish the surest guarantee which can be given that The Sun Mutual Life Insurance Company will continue to confer all the solid benefits of Life Insurance'.

CHANGES AND NEW DIFFICULTIES

There had already been changes among the men who gathered weekly in the Barron Block board room. In 1873 Alexander Buntin declined to stand for re-election. In 1874 Charles J. Coursol retired, to be succeeded by a man who was to loom large in the affairs of the company for the next thirty years. Alexander Walker Ogilvie had been associated from the beginning with the organization of the Sun, and was one of its first shareholders. Head of the great flour-milling business which carried his name, he was, in the course of his long life, to revolutionize milling methods and do much to spur the eastward flow of wheat from the prairies of Manitoba. He was already a considerable figure in finance and public affairs, and had sat for Montreal West in the provincial parliament. Powerful, genial, and engaging, equally at home in English and French, he brought to the Sun not only a prestigious name but a new accession of energy.

New men and new methods were soon to be much in demand. The buoyant young nation in which the company had begun its life was sagging slowly downward into the trough of its first depression. Over-extended and over-confident, with its nineteen new banks and its swollen trade supported by foreign credits, it lay entirely vulnerable to the world outside. From the later months of 1873, panic in the United States and depression in Great Britain and Europe began to be reflected in Canada by called loans, depressed markets, and savage competition from outside products. Shipping and lumbering fell off, factories closed, and retail merchants failed as American merchants dumped their surplus across the border at slaughter prices. For six stagnant years, as the business curve went down, life insurance shared in the time of troubles.

In Great Britain and the United States, companies with inadequate reserves went to the wall, and the reputation of life insurance suffered. Other American companies, hard pressed for business, sent agents into Canada with wildly extravagant terms. Bonuses and rebates of premiums and high-pressure methods of selling went hand in hand with distorted claims and promises until most clients were confused and few agents believed. Added to this there was new pressure, in a steadily constricting market, from perfectly legitimate native competition. The Ontario Mutual, later to be known as The Mutual Life Assurance Company of Canada, had started business in 1870. A year later the Confederation Life Association had been formed, and it was pulling ahead of the Sun. The London Life Insurance Company, in spite of conditions in 1874, entered the field that year; while first still, and still most firmly established, was the veteran, Canada Life.

By the end of 1874, the Sun had 918 policies in force for a total insurance of $1,768,092. The company's assets, including capital, amounted to $151,484, and its income for the year from premiums and interest had been $64,073. 'In view of the very grave questions that are now agitating insurance circles both in England and the United States,' said the statement at the annual meeting, 'it is confidently felt that the prudent course pursued by your Directors will commend itself to the approval of both the Shareholders and the Insured.' The words, true though they might be, had the subdued tone of depression, and the facts justified the tone. Sun's business was sound, but it was not advancing. It was, in fact, declining; and if some of the trouble lay with general conditions there were other factors due to internal flaws.

At the head of operations as Managing Director there was a capable and experienced man. No one doubted the ability of Mathew H. Gault. But he had had competing interests when the Sun was formed, and he had added others later. In 1872 he was one of the founders and had become president of the Exchange Bank of Canada. He was also largely interested in the Montreal Permanent Building Society, which in 1875 was to change its name to the Montreal Loan and Mortgage Company. He was a man with much on his hands at a time when conditions were difficult throughout the whole country, and the growth of the Sun required sustained attention. This Gault could not give, and neither could Thomas Craig, the Secretary, who devoted much of his time to Gault's other affairs. The directors concerned themselves with matters at the centre, but the general work in the field was outside their province. It lay now for the most part on the shoulders of Thomas Gilroy, whom Gault had appointed in 1871 as the company's first Inspector. But Gilroy, though he was to be a valuable and successful official for the next thirty years, could not be everywhere at once and supervise everything. He had found good men scarce, and hard to hold when gained, and few of the early agents were producing anything at all. Two agents had decamped with company funds, most were apathetic and half-trained, and stronger central direction had become a crying need. Gault and the directors, however, were well aware of the problem and had found the man to solve it.

ROBERTSON MACAULAY

He was introduced to the shareholders on March 4, 1875, at the same annual meeting that reviewed the dour tale of the previous year. Robertson Macaulay was then forty-two years old. He had been born in the Scottish highlands at the North Sea port of Fraserburgh, where his father had owned a coasting vessel. From here, after a boyhood coloured by experience of the hard life of the sea, he had gone, at about the age of twelve, to Stornoway in the Hebrides and thence to Aberdeen. He had found work in a dry-goods house and was soon in charge of the records, but they did not hold him long. On January 20, 1854 – his twenty-first birthday – he had taken ship for Canada and passed on to Hamilton with the tide of western immigrants. Here, within two years, the young man with the hands and build of a seaman and some knowledge of bookkeeping had found his life's vocation. Hired as an accountant by Hugh C. Baker, the founder of The Canada Life Assurance Company, he had become the devoted disciple of a convinced pioneer. Hugh C. Baker had believed in life insurance and had fought for it against the thousand doubts and difficulties of a slowly developing country. From him Macaulay acquired, as was to be said years later, 'an absorbing and passionate belief in the rightness of life assurance, a clear conception of its beneficent effects and a burning enthusiasm to enlarge its influence'.

For as long as Baker lived, Macaulay had been a happy man at Canada Life. The succeeding Manager, however, was a Scot much like himself, and there had been a clash of granite temperaments. In 1872 Macaulay resigned from the company and was welcomed in as Secretary by the new Mutual Life Association of Canada. Here he had remained comparatively content for two years, but in June 1874 offers had arrived within a week of each other, one from the Sun Mutual of Montreal and the other from Confederation Life of Toronto. The Sun's offer had come first, and Macaulay had wired his acceptance on the last day of the month. Two weeks later Thomas Craig retired, and on August 2 Robertson Macaulay arrived at the office in the Barron Block to take over the vacant desk. He was now Secretary of the company at a salary of $2,500 per annum, which would be increased to $3,000 if he lasted a second year.

He stood before the shareholders on that March afternoon, a tall, spare, rugged, determined Scot. After seven months in office he was left with few illusions as to the job he had taken on. He had not minced words about the quality of the company's agents, of whom he considered only four to be operative at all. But the company itself was quite another matter. The passionate believer in life insurance, the man with the vocation, had become the man of the Sun, and there was a new era dawning.

3

The Innovator

TO THE FIRST QUINQUENNIUM

It was apparent to the directors at once that they had taken on a formidable man, but the sense of quality too was all-pervasive. The new Secretary, through the first six months of his tenure, had combed the field, stirred up moribund agents, turned the records of the company inside out. He was taking over, with Gault's uneasy concurrence, much of the supervision of daily affairs. His blunt criticisms and flat proposals of change had had almost the force of demands, yet the board had welcomed most of them. Here, for the first time, was the single-minded direction the company had lacked. There were none of the outside interests, none of the distracting worries that were beginning to plague Gault. For Robertson Macaulay the business of life insurance was work and play, meat and drink, and he had given himself to the task of building the Sun. In a field where some twenty-five companies, British, American, and Canadian, were now competing, he meant to drive it to the top.

Of the many problems besetting him, he had seen two as paramount. One was the matter of agencies, and the other the policy itself. They were linked problems, and each was steadily growing under the pressure of hard times. Sketchily-supervised agents, most of them on commission, were unable to make a living and were turning away from the business. And life insurance was not selling because it was not yet what it might be.

At a meeting on December 2, 1874, Macaulay had made known his first partial solutions and had gained the approval of the board. By 1875 the plans were under way. New agents, advertised for, carefully selected by Macaulay and constantly under his eye, were out in the field on salary. They were feeling the spur from Head Office as they had never felt it before, but they were also responding to guidance and the lift of change and improvement. The Secretary, who was everywhere, snapping at faults and pointing out lost opportunities, had also an eye for the difficulties and an ear for good suggestions. He asked much but he gave much, and he was providing better tools.

On February 10, 1875, the Sun entered the accident field with the writing of its first policy. The company's charter permitted the step and the men desired it as an aid to writing life. On February 24 the life policy itself took on a new aspect. A resolution submitted by Macaulay and approved by the directors on that day made a policy indisputable for any cause whatever after having been five years in force. It provided further that 'every possible facility for the maintenance of policies be given by way of loans within their cash value to be applied in payment of premiums'. The day of the modern policy was still far off, but henceforth there would be no claims subject to voidance because of minor technical flaws, and the man in difficulty with his premiums would find the company ready to help him. The results, by the end of 1876, were 'wonderful progress in the face of most unfair and unscrupulous competition from a few American life agents' and a 'marked preference for our combined Life & Accident policy'.

While morale rose in the field, there was also growth and change in administration. On February 9, 1876, the board authorized the engagement of the Honorable Elizur Wright, an eminent Boston actuary, to make a valuation of the company's policies. On the same day Philip S. Ross, the holder of Sun Life Policy No. 35, was appointed as the company's first auditor. His first report, submitted on March 28, 1876, concluded with the following statement:

> Having gone through all this investigation in a thorough manner, it affords me much pleasure in stating that the Books

> are kept in a more correct manner than I usually find books to be which I have been requested to audit. The entries are carefully and correctly made. I am sure that it will give you as much satisfaction as it does me to have this stated.

On this note began a connection which, through succeeding members of the Ross family, has continued to the present day. For ninety-five years the annual statements of Sun Life have been audited by accounting firms bearing the Ross name.

With the close of business in 1876 the Sun reached the term of its fifth full year and the time for the first quinquennial division of profits. The reports of actuary and auditor disclosed a comfortably sound position. Calculating the reserve against policy liabilities at the severe government standard of 4½ per cent, there remained, in addition to paid-up capital, a surplus of $55,299.51. It was distributable, according to the terms of the company's by-laws, in the proportion of 80 per cent to policyholders and 20 per cent to shareholders. The directors, however, were determined to conserve resources and build strength. Of the surplus, only $37,586 was paid out in dividends to the holders of participating policies. An allotment of $12,500 went to increase paid-up capital, and the remainder was held as a reserve against the depreciation of securities.

'T.B.M.'
THE 'MUTUAL' QUESTION

Prudence was still ingrained in the character of the company, and it was still wholly justified by the state of the country round it. The worst years lay ahead. Yet, for the moment, there was a buoyant new sense of confidence and growth. There were five clerks in the office now, and one showed special promise. He was a tall young man who looks out today from one of his early photographs with curiously modern sideburns. He gave the impression to some of being rather frail and shy. When he stood beside Thomas Workman, blotting the President's signature as he signed completed policies, he was sometimes inclined to stutter. He did the office dog-work, being the youngest lad on the staff, but he spent most of his evenings in the study of life insurance. Joining the company at seventeen years of age, on October 2, 1877, he had produced by

1879 'a careful investigation into the cause of death among our insured members'. By 1880 he was assisting the outside actuary, and by 1881 he was to be the Actuary of the company. Thomas Bassett Macaulay, the son of Robertson Macaulay, was already a man to watch.

The Secretary himself, always watchful of everything and always on the move, was encountering new problems and considering new opportunities. He was finding one of his problems in the company name. At a board meeting on February 20, 1878, he caused it to be recorded that 'the term "Mutual" has now become so unpopular in certain parts of the country owing to various failures of Mutual Fire companies and Mutual Benefit or Building societies that attention is requested to the advisability of leaving it from the company's name'. There was no action at the moment and discussion was allowed to lapse, but it signalled change in the future.

THE WEST INDIES

Another and greater problem was the cost of doing business. There was no provision, under the laws of that time, for the preliminary term method of valuing liabilities. Full liability for a policy was assumed from the first year, with no allowance whatever for initial expenses. At the same time, expenses were out of proportion because most agents were now on salary or partial salary and were not yet writing the business to support the amounts paid them. Good men were being held and trained and better and better returns were being produced, yet the very fact of success was creating its own difficulties. The company, in striving for volume against intense competition, was steering a precarious course between the high cost of the business and the high liability assumed. It was the problem of all young companies in the lean Canadian market, and the only effective answer was to find another market.

In the summer of 1879 Macaulay began to look towards the West Indies. Reports told of the islands as an almost virgin field for the writing of life insurance, with only two small local offices doing business and little or no canvassing by the agents of other companies. It was unknown ground to the actuary, and the first of the difficult questions was the rate of mortality. That question was answered little by little as Macaulay with the help of his son began to compile statistics and build up premium tables. Then, with rates established, there remained the question of dealing with prospective business and of finding the man to get it. Tropical business, Macaulay decided, should be kept as a special class on the books of the company, with all profits based on the actual rate of mortality. As to the man, Inspector J. M. C. DelesDerniers had combined a spectacular name with spectacular success as an agent, and was now straining at the leash. Macaulay settled on him for the larger field.

There remained the final matter of convincing the board. On December 3 Macaulay invited consideration of the opening of 'an active connection with the West India Islands'. The directors reacted coolly and were not even certain that the company's charter permitted foreign ventures. This question Macaulay disposed of on December 12, with an opinion from the company's solicitor that the move was quite permissible. There were still doubts, and when the Secretary returned to the attack on the seventeenth the proposal was disapproved. Within two days, however, the wind had abruptly changed. At a meeting on December 19 Mathew H. Gault and Alexander Walker Ogilvie moved to reopen the question, and a lengthy discussion ensued. It was followed by another meeting on December 24, which sanctioned Macaulay's plans and found his table of rates 'abundantly high'. DelesDerniers departed forthwith on a mission of exploration which took him as far as Georgetown, British Guiana. Within a year the company was writing business not only in British Guiana but in Trinidad and Tobago, Barbados, Antigua, St. Kitts, Dominica, Grenada, St. Lucia, Montserrat, St. Vincent, Jamaica, the Bahamas, and Martinique. The aggressive DelesDerniers, though he and the Sun were not to be long in company, was strewing the seed of enormous future growth, and the directors were duly appreciative. When he complained of his difficulties in moving about with sufficient speed, the board decided 'to buy him a carriage here, and after using it at Jamaica to sell it again'.

THE FIRST INTERNAL STRAINS

With its expansion to the West Indies in 1879 Sun Life took its first step towards the stature of a world-wide institution. Yet it entered in the same year on a long, unhappy period of strain and crisis. On January 29, 1879, Mathew H. Gault announced that he was resigning as Managing Director. On March 31 the resignation was accepted. The reason given was that Gault had been offered the position of manager for Canada of a British insurance company and could not, therefore, continue as Manager of the Sun. There were other reasons, however, of which the directors were painfully aware.

Hard times, as usual, were impressing their hard lessons on over-extended men. The Exchange Bank of Canada and the Montreal Loan and Mortgage Company were both in serious difficulties. On August 7, after three closings by other Montreal banks, the Exchange Bank suspended payment. It reopened on November 3, without loss to depositors, but with confidence seriously impaired. At the same time the strength of the mortgage company was also dwindling. As the head of both concerns, Gault was heavily involved; and a matter of greater moment was the involvement of the Sun.

On June 17, 1874, the company at Gault's suggestion had subscribed for $30,000 of the stock of the Montreal Permanent Building Society, which was now known as the Montreal Loan and Mortgage Company. In April and May of 1875 it had invested $10,000 in shares of the Exchange Bank. Both investments at the time had seemed choice and had had the full concurrence of the board. By 1878, however, there had begun to be serious doubts; and at the close of business in 1879 the stocks stood written down by a total of $14,518.

It was against this background that Gault had retired from the active management of the Sun. Neither he nor the other directors were yet aware of the full gravity of the position. Alexander Walker Ogilvie, who was a director of the Exchange Bank, remained confident that it would recover the ground lost. Gault, as a man who had many irons in the fire, had depended heavily on Thomas Craig, his brother-in-law, the former Secretary of the company. Craig, on leaving the Sun, had become manager of the mortgage company and then, in replacement of an absconding predecessor, the Cashier of the Exchange Bank. He seems always to have convinced his busy superiors that he was a sound and safe executive.

He had, however, not convinced Robertson Macaulay. The new Secretary of the Sun had been concerned from the beginning, not only with the soundness of the Exchange Bank and of the Montreal

Loan and Mortgage Company, but with the fact that such investments had been made at all. They represented in his eyes the use of the funds of policyholders to support directors' interests. To the outraged directors it was another thing entirely. They were all substantial men, as proud of their reputations as of their wealth. They risked their own money in the various concerns they controlled, and administered the funds of investors with the same care and judgment. They considered this to be their function with the funds of the Sun Mutual Life. Macaulay, however, demanded more than that. Life insurance, to him, was a specialized, specially responsible field in which ordinary business practice was not enough. There could be no risk and no investment made where the directors' private interests were concerned at all. It was a new doctrine and a stern doctrine in the Canadian commercial world of the 1870s, and it boded future conflict.

For the moment the sinking shares were worry enough. The crucial issue had been hardly raised. Mathew Gault moved his office from the Barron Block and the Sun's staff took over the vacant space. The former Managing Director, with the warm concurrence of his colleagues, remained a member of the board. On September 10, 1879, following the resignation of T. James Claxton, he was elected Vice-President. For all his mounting differences with Robertson Macaulay, it was Gault with Ogilvie who resurrected the West Indies project at the meeting of December 19. At the same meeting he joined with the other directors in the unanimous agreement by which Robertson Macaulay became Manager of the company as well as Secretary.

So far as business was concerned the new year seemed to open with considerable promise. The company went on with increasing vigour in the field. The move to the West Indies had now been launched, and another and greater decision was close at hand. Yet overhanging the future was the prospect of heavy loss; and for the first time in the central direction of the company there was basic disagreement.

4

'The Sun Is Setting'

THE UNCONDITIONAL POLICY

At a presentation ceremony on January 9, 1906, Robertson Macaulay, the seventy-two-year-old President of the Sun Life Assurance Company of Canada, was moved by the eulogies of his staff to indulge in reminiscence. 'In no square, stand-up fight,' he said, 'have I ever acknowledged defeat, but once. That was in the Wright case, when Wrong triumphed. My inner soul rebelled, but redress came from a very unlooked-for quarter – the Unconditional Policy.'

He was looking back by then, with a certain mellow detachment, across more than a quarter of a century. At the time of which he spoke, however, he was faced with the crowding troubles of 1880. One of the crucial developments in the history of the company came at a period when Sun Life, still struggling against depressed external conditions and dangerous internal dissension, was also faced with the consequences of a serious defeat at law. It could hardly have seemed a time for adventurous change. Yet the change was made and it was basic, and the result was a widening of horizons for all life insurance.

The principal in the Wright case, which Macaulay remembered so vividly, was a man who held one of the company's early accident policies. In December 1875 the company was presented with a death claim which, in Macaulay's opinion, was based not only on suicide but on clearly evident conspiracy in the taking out of the policy. The claim was refused and the case went to the courts, but in April 1878 in the face of what Macaulay regarded as overwhelming evidence a jury found for the plaintiff. The acts and motives of the insured, and the terms of the policy itself, were equally ignored. Whatever the man's intentions, and whatever the mass of restrictions hedging him round, to the twelve men in the box the issue was clear. A man had been insured, and he had died. The large corporation, faceless and always suspect, should be made to pay.

For two years thereafter, though the company fought the settlement to the last ditch, it was more concerned with the problems raised by the verdict. The claim had been against an accident policy, but the result affected life policies too. All policies were protected by equivalent sets of conditions, and all protection was valueless if the precedent established by the Wright case should come to be generally applied. In the case of suicide, in the case of a man engaged in a forbidden occupation, in the case of a man residing in a part of the world where he was not covered under the conditions of the policy, what was the likely prospect? The prospect was that restrictions would be ignored, that in spite of the terms of its contract the company would be forced to pay. It would contest a claim with little hope of winning and with the clear certainty of prejudicing itself in the eyes of the general public.

Other considerations began to rise. While the various 'thou-shalt-nots' were proving ineffective, they were also a bar to selling. 'At that time,' as the son of Robertson Macaulay was to say years later, 'our insurance policies were compared to the Grand Trunk bills of lading because of the mass of small-type conditions on the back.' Few prospects read them but too many were repelled by them, and they failed to protect the company when put to the test. The answer seemed to be to dispense with them all.

It was a hard answer, and a long time in coming. It involved a revolution in traditional thinking. On May 5, 1880, however, the directors came to their decision. The new forms of the Unconditional Policy went out to the agents. The back was cleared of the small type and the face of the policy carried three crisp sentences:

> The assured may reside in any part of the world without extra premium.
>
> The assured may engage in any occupation without extra premium.
>
> This policy will be *indisputable* on any ground whatever after it has been in force for two full years.

No insurance company in the world, at that time, was offering such a policy. There was a 'world-wide' policy offered by a Scottish company which was practically free of conditions, but Macaulay desired more. In his view the very essence of the change was that it applied at the usual premiums to all acceptable risks. He found no company in North America to share the view, and there were many warnings of loss and disaster ahead. Yet he had opened a road that the others would have to follow, until the unconditional policy became part of insurance law. In the meantime, for the jubilant agents of the Sun, there was a new and unique opportunity which they very quickly grasped. 'Our canvassers,' said Thomas Bassett Macaulay, who was an eager watcher of the process, 'used to merely open out the policy of any competitor, then open out ours, point to the mass of conditions in the one and their absence in the other and ask, "Which do you prefer?"'

CHANGE OF NAME

Through the next half-dozen years, with the unconditional policy contributing mightily, the volume of business grew. The scope widened. The first two small annuity contracts were written in 1880. In Manitoba and in British Columbia, where the company had gained some foothold in the early seventies, it now began to expand. In 1881 it took the step foreshadowed three years earlier by petitioning for a change of name; and on May 17, 1882, with the formal assent of Parliament, it became the Sun Life Assurance Company of Canada.

THE CRISIS AND THE CONCLUSION

The amount of insurance in force at the end of 1887 was $10,873,777. In that single year the agents of Sun Life had written over three and a quarter millions of new business, which was more than the total in force a decade earlier. Operations were flourishing in the West Indies and were now extended coast-to-coast in Canada. Yet the company was only emerging, if it had yet fully emerged, from the throes of an inner conflict that had threatened to bring it down. 'The Sun Is Setting' had been a headline in one of the commercial newspapers in 1885, and the dire prediction had seemed at the time almost justified.

The crisis had been building steadily since the suspension and reopening of the Exchange Bank in 1879. It came to a peak in September 1883, with the bank's total failure. Thomas Craig's management had contributed to the final wreck, but Gault and Ogilvie who had trusted him were deeply involved too. So were the fortunes of the Montreal Loan and Mortgage Company which, though it survived the crisis, was all too closely linked with the bank's affairs. On December 29, 1883, Robertson Macaulay confronted the board with the results to Sun Life.

He had been urging for years that the stock in the bank and the mortgage company both be sold. Instead, the holdings in the mortgage company had been almost doubled. The investment in the Exchange Bank was shown now at a value of $8,850, and in the mortgage company at $64,200. The bank shares had become a total write-off and carried in addition a double liability which would reach a further $5,000. The stock of the mortgage company was certainly of doubtful value, very likely unsaleable on the present market, and might be a total loss if the company failed. There was a maximum possible loss, in view of all contingencies, of some $78,000. It represented, on the books of Sun Life, more than the prospective surplus for the year just closing. It promised impairment of capital and the loss of public confidence that would be the sure prelude to ruin.

He spoke now as Managing Director of the company, for he had been elected to the board on November 27. But he was untamed by the honour, and he had a grim proposal for his colleagues. Of the bank he said nothing, for there was nothing more to be said. On the mortgage company, however, his views were clear. Whether the stock was a good investment or a bad investment it should never have been made at all, since it involved the private interests of certain directors. It had proved to be a bad investment. It threatened the very existence of Sun Life, and it would certainly decrease the dividends to the holders of participating policies. For this the men responsible should be prepared to accept the consequences. They should buy back the stock and assume the loss themselves.

The half-revealed division of four years earlier was now fully surfaced. A stormy board-room argument went on through a second meeting two days later. The directors flared at the implied reflection on their acts. They had used their best judgment, as they did with all investments, and with that their responsibility came to an end. Mathew H. Gault, the man in the eye of the storm, had offered his resignation the previous March. He sat at the table now, already ailing, with less than four years to live. Andrew Gault, his brother, who had missed the first meeting, stalked into the second with an angry threat to resign. Alexander Walker Ogilvie, the Gaults' firmest supporter, rejected Macaulay's argument and the premise on which it was based. He was convinced that the stock of the mortgage company, though perhaps at a slight discount, was still good value. But he was not prepared to be bludgeoned into purchasing it, and neither were any of his colleagues. There was no resolution of differences as they walked out of the board room on the last day of the year.

On January 3, 1884, the resignation of Andrew Frederick Gault was in the hands of the directors. On the fifteenth it was returned to him, declined as his brother's had been the previous March. Through February, as clerks and auditor worked on the annual statement, there was a kind of sultry peace. At a meeting on March 4, however, the battle renewed itself on a wider front.

Robertson Macaulay, who had had his one defeat in a square, stand-up fight, was not prepared to accept the loss of a second. The policy rift was basic, and there was no papering it over. Either he or the opposing directors would have to go. The board demurred; the company was in no condition to change the names at its masthead. For Macaulay, the condition of the company was what made the change necessary. He named the brothers Gault, and Alexander Walker Ogilvie. The members of the board, however, though they wavered on two of the suggestions, were firmly united against him in support of Mathew H. Gault.

By March 11, with the statement for 1883 now prepared, there had come a change of mood. The routine business of the meeting was dispatched with cool formality. Macaulay was then requested by the President, Thomas Workman, to step out of the room for a time. He returned to find that Mathew Gault was gone, and to be informed that his resignation would soon be submitted to the board. As to Andrew Gault and Ogilvie, the position remained equivocal; but with this the directors parted.

They met at the annual meeting two days later, to present the shareholders with a statement from which the stock of the Exchange Bank had disappeared. The stock of the Montreal Loan and Mortgage Company was to dwindle on the books for another twenty years. For the year 1883 it was shown at a value of $36,000 among the assets supporting a precarious surplus of $20,841.44. The position was hardly a comfortable one, there were few congratulations, and the only immediate sequel was a sharp rebuff for Macaulay. Andrew Frederick Gault succeeded his brother as Vice-President, and Alexander Walker Ogilvie retained his seat on the board. The hope of recouping any loss to policyholders seemed finally laid to rest.

The likelier prospect seemed to be that Robertson Macaulay would go. He made it clear that he was still unchanged in his views, and the directors remained as ominously firm in theirs. For two years, as the company climbed laboriously towards safer ground, the challenge of the next quinquennium loomed ahead. It would come at the end of 1886 and at that time, as Macaulay had plainly indicated, the major question at issue would be settled once and for all. A mistake in investment policy would be set right, and it would be set right retroactively. Not only would there be no further investments in concerns controlled by directors; the loss on such previous investments would be returned from shareholders' profits.

To this, in the view of Andrew Gault, Alexander Walker Ogilvie, and several of the other directors and large shareholders, there was only one answer. It began to take shape towards the end of 1886. At a meeting on November 30, the Managing Director informed the board that according to his information Andrew Frederick Gault was endeavouring to obtain the proxies of shareholders and directors for some unexplained reason. The matter was discussed perfunctorily and allowed to drop, for it was hardly news to anyone. It was, indeed, a topic of lively discussion, not only in the Barron Block office but among the agents in the field.

Through the winter of 1886-7 a proxy battle of Homeric proportions developed. It still centred around the familiar issue and would still be decided in the dark and cramped little board room of which the directors had been complaining since 1878, but the personnel was changing. Mathew Gault, the founder of the company, was gone; he was to die in June of 1887. Thomas Workman still presided at the table, but of the other original directors only Andrew Gault remained. He was certain of the support of Alexander Walker Ogilvie, and many of the newer directors leaned his way. Only Samuel H. Ewing, a future vice-president, and James Tasker, a prominent businessman who had just begun a quarter-century with the board, inclined to Macaulay's side. It seemed probable that the Managing Director, at fifty-four years of age, would soon be departing in search of other employment.

By mid-February, however, a change in the wind was felt. Ewing and Tasker were not the only ones among the directors and large shareholders who had begun to be impressed with the force of Macaulay's views. The agents in the field were all solidly behind him. Some of them were shareholders and all of them went to work on other shareholders with the skill of persuasive men, thoroughly convinced. Little by little, the count of Macaulay's proxies began to rise.

At a board meeting on February 22, 1887, the Managing Director made known the proposal he intended to advance. It was that the proportion of the quinquennial surplus distributable to shareholders should be reduced from 20 per cent to 10 per cent and the difference made over to policyholders. The reason was 'that the serious losses from investments during the current quinquennium will greatly diminish the rate hitherto paid to assured participating members'. It was a flat rebuke to the board's policies of previous years, a flat warning that such policies must change. And it was given now with confidence. The meeting three days later was anticlimactic. Andrew F. Gault listened impassively as Macaulay's motion was passed, rose and walked from the board room. On March 16 he resigned.

The issue had turned on a matter of some $9,000 at most, the difference between 10 and 20 per cent of the distributable surplus. Few were concerned at all with the thought of the money. Yet more was at stake than a war of personalities. The decision involved not only the direction of the company but its character. It would affect the course to be followed in the investment of billions of dollars of the funds of future policyholders. And that course had been set now by the tall, hard-faced Scot.

5

Widening Horizons

THE SECOND PRESIDENT AND THE NEW HOME

Of the original directorate of Sun Life, only Thomas Workman, the President, now remained. For sixteen years, though never directly concerned with the management of affairs, he had been a dominant figure in the board room. He had stood above though not remote from the storms, and his cool, resilient strength was one of the great assets now. Respected by all and liked by all, he had come to accept the force of Macaulay's views. Yet he also held the regard of Macaulay's opponents. Alexander Walker Ogilvie, tough, powerful, and resentful, might well have left the company in the wake of the Gaults. He did not; he stayed to become Vice-President under Workman. It was clear at first that he stayed in the hope of succeeding him, yet that was soon to change. In the last two years of the aging President's life, as peace returned to the board room and the company surged forward, Ogilvie came to appreciate the quality of its new direction. In the autumn of 1889 Thomas Workman died. It was on a motion of Alexander Walker Ogilvie, unanimously passed at the board meeting of October 15, 1889, that Robertson Macaulay became President and Managing Director of Sun Life.

The new President, at the annual meeting for 1889, delivered a promise that was glowingly fulfilled on May 1, 1891. On that day the books, records, equipment, and the twenty-two members of the Head Office staff of Sun Life moved out of the quarters in the Barron Block to the company's first real home. It was a five-storey building erected at a corner site on Notre Dame Street adjoining St. Alexis and Hospital streets, and its completion was an event in the city. The directors, having decided that building was cheaper than renting, had elected for something 'modest, not pretentious . . . in keeping with the company's character'. As was always to be their way, however, they had not neglected details or pinched pennies when once resolved on a project. The building justified their careful selection of an architect and the $175,000 spent on it. It was the first fireproof steel-frame construction in Montreal, it boasted the first electric elevator and its offices, according to one admiring newspaper, were finished 'in solid cherry in bank style, with every modern luxury and convenience'. It was to be succeeded later in the decade by other handsome buildings in Sherbrooke, Hamilton, and Ottawa, but this was the first and finest. It stood up, that May morning, a solid, convincing testimony to regained strength and confidence. The Sun had weathered its storms now, and the problems lying ahead were the problems of growth.

THE MACAULAYS AND THE FAR EAST

They would be problems largely resolved, through the next quarter of a century, by the efforts of two men. Thomas Bassett Macaulay was now Secretary of Sun Life, as well as Actuary. He had been elected to the post just two weeks after his father became President, and the title had only confirmed what had long been fact. The man just entering his thirties was a guiding force in the company, a strong support to his father and sometimes a thorn in his side. The team was all the stronger for its occasional internal strains, and it was not always the younger man who pushed the older on. The 'Dear Tom' of yellowing letters in the files is sometimes pleading the conservative view against 'My Dear Father'. Yet whichever party yielded in the course of vigorous debate, it was always a joint decision that emerged. It was a decision carried forward with single-minded purpose, and the dimensions of that purpose were now about to be revealed.

The company, as it entered the last decade of the century, was healthy in the home field and flourishing in the West Indies. Sometimes as much as $60,000 in applications came from the Caribbean in a single mail. Yet the problems that had led to the first adventure abroad were only recurring now on a larger scale. The pace of growth could not be maintained in Canada. The population was still too small and scattered; competition was too keen. Nor were the West Indies enough to redress the balance. There must either be a slowing-down or a search for a wider field.

There is no record of the long colloquies between father and son, or the long nights of study and investigation that must have preceded action. Thomas Bassett Macaulay, however, was ready for action by 1891. 'One day,' recorded Ira B. Thayer, who was then Superintendent of Agencies, 'he sent for me and, pointing to a map of the Orient, said, "We believe that there is a great field for life insurance in the Far East, but we do not know. We want you to go there and find out."'

The words were the start of an odyssey that was to carry Thayer by way of Vancouver to Yokohama and the other principal cities of Japan, from there to China, the Straits Settlements, India, and Ceylon, and from there round the world home, with flying visits to Egypt and Palestine on the way. He was gone almost a year, and within a few months of his return James S. Snasdell was consolidating the ground he had gained and extending it in the East Indies. Meanwhile, from the first bases in the West Indies, the search for new business, under James C. Tory and W. A. Higinbotham, was proceeding through Central America down the west coast of South America. By 1899 it had widened to include Africa, and H. B. Higinbotham, a younger brother of the first man, was embarked on a journey down the long east coast of the continent. He had reached Cape Town and travelled inland to Johannesburg when the outbreak of war in South Africa brought that mission to a pause.

The great work of expansion had been begun at a time when the British Empire was at the peak of its power and influence. It had been done by picked men who were alive to their opportunities. Thayer was a force in the company for six years, Snasdell and the Higinbothams were all three to rise high in its ranks, and James C. Tory, in addition to becoming a director, was a future Lieutenant-Governor of Nova Scotia. Wherever these men had gone, armed

The entire Head Office staff – January 1887. T. B. Macaulay and Robertson Macaulay first and second from right, seated.

Architect's sketch of the new Head Office Building on Notre Dame Street, 1891.

A typical Sun Life agents' outing, 1899.

CLASS E.
"UNCONDITIONAL POLICY."

THE

SUN MUTUAL LIFE INSURANCE COMPANY OF MONTREAL

Sum Assured, $1000. Age, 26. Years.

Incorporated by Act of the Parliament of the Dominion of Canada.

L.P. of Par.

No. 6549.

1/2 Yearly Premium, $12 80/100 For 20 Years.

In Consideration of the representations, agreements and stipulations contained in the Application for this Policy, and of the sum of Twelve 80/100 Dollars, to be to them duly paid, on the first day of April 1881, as a premium for six calendar months, and of the payment of a like amount on the first day of October next, and half yearly thereafter, on the same date in every year during the continuance of this Policy or until Twenty full years' Premiums shall have been paid.

THIS COMPANY

Do Hereby Assure the life of Franklin Nash (signing "Frank Nash") of Cornwall, Province of Ontario, Machinist, in the sum of One Thousand Dollars, with participation in the profits of the said Company.

And the said Company hereby bind themselves to pay the said amount of Assurance in lawful money current in Canada, at their Chief Office, in the City of Montreal, to the Assured's Assigns, or to his Legal Representatives, within sixty days after due notice, and proof (satisfactory to the Board of Directors) of the death of the said Franklin Nash shall have been received at the said Office, in Montreal, Canada; the balance of the year's Premium, if any, being first deducted therefrom.

In Witness Whereof, the said Company have hereunto affixed their Seal, and caused these Presents to be signed by their President and Manager and Secretary, at Montreal, this twenty third day of March, one thousand eight hundred and eighty one.

Examined: R.J.

R. Macaulay
Manager and Secretary.

Thomas Workman
President.

PRIVILEGES.

1st.—The assured may reside in any part of the world without extra Premium.

2nd.—The assured may engage in any occupation without extra Premium.

3rd.—Thirty days of grace are allowed for the payment of renewal Premiums.

4th.—This Policy may be revived at any time within twelve months from the date of lapse, on production of a certificate of health, satisfactory to the Directors, and payment of whatever revival fine may be imposed (not exceeding 10 per cent. of the Premiums in arrear). in addition to the Premiums overdue.

5th.—After the payment of Premiums for three or more full years, the Company will, if requested, and on the surrender of this Policy duly receipted, issue a Commuted Policy in exchange therefor, for as many twentieth parts of the sum Assured as there shall have been Complete annual Premiums received, on which no further Premium shall be required; provided, application for such Paid-up Policy be made in writing within two months from the lapse of this Policy.

6th.—Loans will be made by the Company when desired, to assist in keeping the Policy in force, after it has been two years in existence.

7th.—This Policy will be *indisputable*, on any ground whatever, after it has been in force for two full years, if the Premiums hereunder are regularly paid. If the age has been unintentionally understated, the difference in Premium resulting therefrom, with interest, must be paid; if overstated, an allowance will be made therefor.

8th.—If any difference arise with regard to this Policy, such difference may be submitted to the arbitration of two persons—one to be appointed by the claimant, the other by the Directors—whose award, or that of the umpire whom they may appoint, shall be binding and conclusive.

The new 'Unconditional' Policy form as issued in 1881.

Robertson Macaulay, second President, 1889-1915.

only with letters of introduction, policy applications, and their own zest and intelligence, they had been able to write business and to find reputable agents. They had been able to adapt to the laws and customs of the countries and they had come back with a knowledge of the ways of varying peoples which would be priceless to the company later. They had justified the hope of the Macaulays that there was a need and desire for life insurance and, that being established, they had been guided with a loose rein. 'When your work in the Eastern Mediterranean is finished,' ran one casual instruction, 'strike down the Red Sea for the east coast of Africa. . . . You can, if you think well of it, run over to Madagascar. You should certainly take in Mauritius. After leaving Cape Colony, take coasting steamers, again stopping at every little settlement on the west coast, but don't go up the Congo. In this way you will in time reach Senegal.' In this way, by the end of the nineteenth century, Sun Life had reached very far indeed. It was known and it was doing business not only in the West Indies, but in treaty ports, inland cities, and even the hinterland of the Orient and the Far East, in parts of Africa and the Near East, on the Central American mainland, and in South America as far south as Punta Arenas on the Straits of Magellan, then the most southerly town in the world.

THE UNITED KINGDOM

It was also, by that time, firmly established in England and the United States. On May 13, 1893, Thayer, the first round-the-world emissary, had taken ship for London with a party of four. He and his colleagues were to establish an office in London, largely as a result of Thayer's previous work. He had found on his tour of the Orient that many of his prospective policyholders were men with their roots in England. Businessmen, government officials, traders and travellers alike, they were all somehow part of the expanding Empire, looking to retirement at home when their work was done. 'What is the address of your London office?' had been a frequent first question, and the reply that a British bank acted as collecting agent had been less than satisfactory. Now, as much for prestige abroad as in the hope of British business, it had been decided to give the Sun of Canada a London address.

Neither the place chosen nor the address itself was particularly impressive, and disaster threatened the enterprise almost at once. Number 42 Poultry, E.C., though it was near the Bank of England, was a small, second-floor office over a shop, reached by a narrow staircase. Here Thayer, with the 'lightning canvassers' he had brought from Canada – Robert Junkin, Holland A. White, Albert Edward Donovan, and Edward Willans – established the first London office of the Sun Life Assurance Company of Canada. Their literature began to appear wearing the device of the company, which represented Phoebus driving the chariot of the sun. But they had hardly prepared to do battle with the giant insurance companies of the British Isles when one of the giants struck. It was Thayer's unpleasant duty to report to Robertson Macaulay that the Sun Life Assurance Society, which had been doing business in England for eighty years, demanded that the Canadian interloper abandon its name and emblem.

Macaulay's reply came back, 'Fight it', and later instructions ordered the engagement of 'the best counsel in England'. The best counsel, however, was on his way to a judgeship, and was retained only briefly before he ascended the bench. 'Sir Horace Davey,' came the glum report from London, 'examined the brief, said he did not know whether we could win or not, and charged us £79 for that opinion.' Sun Life of Canada remained firm in its own view, and Robertson Macaulay arrived in England to support it. The case, pleaded for the Sun of Canada by another eminent barrister, came to an amicable settlement in 1894. Though fully upheld in the right to use its name, the company agreed to forgo the use of its emblem. It further agreed that in the British Isles, to differentiate it from the other company, its title 'Sun Life of Canada' or 'Sun of Canada' would always be used. 'I believe,' said the presiding judge, 'that the company is here to trade on its own reputation and . . . that it has a perfect right to do so.'

The British company, once the decision was given, accepted it and was soon on a friendly basis with its Canadian rival. Sun of Canada, well advertised by successful litigation, was off to a running start in the British Isles. In the annual report for 1897 it was able to announce that the Most Hon. the Marquess of Dufferin and Ava, the Right Hon. the Earl of Albemarle and Sir Charles Dalrymple, Bart., M.P., had consented to act as trustees of securities deposited by the company with the Bank of Scotland for the protection of policyholders in Great Britain. These notable names, particularly that of Dufferin and Ava, who had been

Governor General of Canada and Viceroy of India, were impressive proof of the standing already gained.

By the turn of the century, with agencies in London, Manchester, Newcastle, Southampton, and Bradford, in Aberdeen, Edinburgh, and Glasgow, and in Dublin and Belfast, Sun Life was also established in France, Holland, and Belgium. The operations on the continent, however, were cramped by restrictive laws and were never to become very large. Of much greater consequence was the decision to enter the United States.

THE UNITED STATES

James C. Tory had come home from the West Indies in 1894 and was being urged by the Macaulays to take over the business in the Orient. He demurred at that, and was offered an alternative proposal. Great American insurance companies were doing a sizable business in Canada, some of it, undoubtedly, at the expense of Sun Life. It was perfectly fair competition and nobody could complain, but it had turned the thoughts of management towards that huge American market. If the giants looked north, could not smaller companies look south? It would certainly be an interesting experiment, and Tory was invited to attempt it.

This proposal he accepted and in November 1895, under Tory's management, Sun Life opened its first American office in the city of Detroit. It had chosen the state of Michigan for a number of good reasons. Michigan was centrally situated in the United States. Its territory adjoined Ontario, one of the most heavily populated and prolific territories of Sun Life. Many of the people of Michigan were of British or Canadian stock, or were acquainted with Canadian ways. A considerable number of businessmen whose interest spanned the border were acquainted with Sun Life. It was perhaps rash to challenge the American companies on their home ground, but it was not so rash in Michigan as it might have been elsewhere.

The company, too, entered the United States with a number of solid advantages which were soon to become apparent. Not least were its reputation and the reputation of Canada. Canadian insurance laws were recognized at that time as being the best in the world. No policyholder in a Canadian life company had ever lost a dollar guaranteed by his policy, as none has to this day. And Sun

Life, with its Scots management and its name for liberal settlements, was now approaching the lead among Canadian insurance companies.

Once again, here as in Canada, the unconditional policy proved its worth. Many of the American policies still carried the old restrictive conditions. On the face of the Sun's policy these restrictions were waived. And on the back now, laid out in columns for the benefit of sceptical prospects, was a new table of values that reflected another advance. In 1894, by means of an automatic non-forfeiture provision, the company had extended its protection of the man in arrears with his premiums. It had long recognized that policies often lapsed because of simple neglect or ignorance; the man who neglected to pay neglected to apply for a loan. Now, after a policy had been two years in force, the necessity of applying for a loan was done away with. The reserve value of the policy became available automatically to be applied to premiums due. The table showed not only these values as they accumulated annually, but the cash loan values based on the reserve and the value of paid-up insurance. The prospect saw in advance, as an absolute guarantee, the full worth of his investment as it built up year by year.

The Sun was once more leading the way in North America towards insurance practices that would receive the endorsement of law a few years later. In the meantime, James C. Tory was the man to take advantage of his opportunities. So was his younger brother, John A. Tory, who succeeded him as Manager for Michigan in 1897; while in the same year the seasoned W. A. Higinbotham arrived from South America. Between them, through the last five years of the century, they not only consolidated the company's base in Michigan but built up a powerful field force that invaded ten more states. The Sun Life, by 1900, was established and doing business in Michigan, Utah, North Carolina, South Carolina, New Jersey, Pennsylvania, Virginia, Wyoming, Maryland, Montana, and Georgia.

EXPANSION AND RE-DIRECTION

The operations of the company, since Thayer took ship in 1891, had become world-wide in scope. The advances of the decade had been enormous, and the first decision crucial. 'Had the Sun Life of Canada adopted the policy of remaining solely within the limits of the Dominion,' said Arthur B. Wood, a later President of the company, in 1922, 'we should not today be occupying the proud position of the largest life assurance company of Canada . . . we would still be trailing along in a respectable second place . . . [with] about one half of the business in force that we actually have now upon our books.'

In domestic affairs, meanwhile, the company had made advances and changes. In 1889, with the institution of the liened policy, the insurance began of under-average lives. In 1890, with the acquisition of the business of the Citizens Insurance Company of Canada, amounting to $1.8 million, came a first venture in the field of 'bulk reinsurance', which was the assumption of liability for policies originally written by another company. It was to become an important aspect of later growth. On January 1, 1893, in order to concentrate on its main function, Sun Life transferred all its existing accident business to the Canada Accident Assurance Company, which undertook to carry out all contracts to the letter. 'Let us develop life assurance,' said T. B. Macaulay.

The 'Thrift Plan', launched in 1895, was an effort to reach the wage-earner in the lower ranks of industry. The company was not prepared to set up the organization and adopt the system of weekly premiums used by most industrial life insurance companies, but it did feel that a modification was possible. After a good deal of study it advanced a plan which offered policies to a maximum of $500 on which no medical examination was required and on which premiums were payable quarterly. Though the experiment seemed promising at first, it was to be abandoned in 1910. Fifteen years of experience were to show that the house-to-house canvassing and the work of premium collection involved a disproportionate amount of the agent's time and sometimes checked his development as a writer of ordinary business. In the meantime, however, the company was widening its scope and preaching its gospel of life insurance among people of smaller incomes who would be a great market of the future.

In the year 1900 the company wrote $10.5 million of new business, and its total insurance in force reached the amount of $58 million. Its assets had increased six times over since 1889 and now stood at $10,486,891. It offered to its policyholders, not only an impressive picture of strength and growth, but a record of increasing profits in which they were sharing to the full. The 90 per cent of profits which they had received in 1887 had been increased to 93⅓ per cent in 1892, and again in 1897 to 95 per cent. The company could now claim, with little exaggeration, that it 'provided the safety of a Stock company with the profits of a Mutual one'.

There were now seventy people on the staff at Head Office, and one of them was Arthur B. Wood, the man who was to succeed the Macaulays at the head of the company. A gold medallist in mathematics at McGill University, he had been teaching at St. Johns, Quebec, when Dr. Henry Marshall Tory recommended him as a likely prospect for an assistant to T. B. Macaulay. An offer of $700 a year brought Wood to Sun Life in 1893, and by 1900 he had advanced from chief clerk to the post of Assistant Actuary.

Miss Kate Andrews, who began her career with Sun Life on May 11, 1894, was the first of many women at Head Office who would serve long and well. *Sunshine,* the company's first magazine, was launched in 1896, and in the same year the first of the 'Agency Outings', at Bobcaygeon, Ontario, brought men from the field and men from Head Office together for a lively session of fishing and fun and shop talk. To the Macaulays, father and son, always at home with agents and fond of the outdoors, it was a great and useful occasion; and the annual outings at various centres across the country became another of Sun Life's traditions.

The new building on Notre Dame Street was still ample for the staff and for the company's various tenants. But the future had to be thought of. In 1897 the company had acquired the adjoining Waddell building and two years later it had purchased the building known as Trafalgar Chambers, to the rear, across Hospital Street. Now, with Trafalgar Chambers connected to the main building by a bridge over the street, Sun Life considered itself accommodated for a good many years ahead.

In 1897, the year of Queen Victoria's Diamond Jubilee, the company proposed to recognize the great occasion by erecting a suitable memorial. By happy coincidence, the location agreed on with the City of Montreal was a site on Dominion Square, facing Dorchester Street. Here, on May 24, 1898, the 'Diamond Jubilee Fountain', a handsome pile of granite surmounted by the figure of a lion couchant and bearing a series of plaques commemorating historical figures and events, was unveiled and dedicated. Fifteen years later, though there had been no thought of it in 1898, the Head Office building of Sun Life began to rise on the site across from Dominion Square. Change came again with the widening of Dorchester Street in 1953. It became necessary to move the monument, which had ceased to be a fountain; and the new location, some 150 feet to the northeast, placed the lion on his pile almost exactly face to face with the main entrance of the Sun Life building.

All this was far in the future as the new century came on, but the promise of change was everywhere. Canada was already embarked upon the great era of progress that would continue to the First World War. Immigration was flooding in, transforming life in the east and quickening the western prairies. It meant great new opportunities, new dimensions of thinking, new uses for money. For Sun Life, with the large investment funds with which it was now beginning to be confronted, it meant reconsideration of former investment policies. Throughout the nineties, after the storms of the eighties, investment had come to be confined largely to mortgages and municipal bonds. Safety had been the great factor, but it was not the only factor. There was also the duty of putting money to work with the greatest possible advantage both to the policyholder and the country. And that duty, as it was now coming to be realized, pointed in a new direction.

There was already thinking along lines that would be clearly laid out in the annual report for 1901. 'The reading of the business horoscope,' said that report, 'indicates the imminence of a vast movement towards the utilization of our immense water-power, water-ways, mineral wealth, agricultural lands, pulpwood forests, and almost unlimited prairies; and in the development of inland and maritime shipping and commercial and industrial pursuits. That would mean the investment of vast sums of money in industrial improvements.'

T. B. Macaulay, speaking in 1901, paralleled this thinking. Railway bonds, by the end of the nineteenth century, had come to be accepted as another field of investment, but it would be wise to look beyond them. 'The latter half of the nineteenth century,' he said, 'has been termed the age of steam, but the indications are numerous that the first half of this century will be the age of electricity. We will do well to ask ourselves whether the securities of some of the corporations which depend upon this new and rising power may not be just as desirable as those which depend upon the power which has already reached its zenith.'

Sun Life, in its investment policy, was approaching a new decision.

6

The Rising Sun

DIFFICULTIES OF GROWTH

'Life assurance,' said T. B. Macaulay, 'is not merely noteworthy for its beneficence . . . it is also the most intricate and technical of all financial systems.' He was speaking in 1907, in the midst of new problems, but the words had equal force at the turn of the century. The man who looked onward had also to look inward at the complex workings of the company. It was the intricacies and technicalities of a steadily expanding business, as well as broad conditions in the world around it, that were bringing the need of change.

One of the continuing anomalies was the tug between strength and growth. Always interdependent, they sometimes seemed in conflict, and it was a matter of constant difficulty to maintain both together. New business meant new revenues, but it also meant new liabilities and required additional reserves. It added little immediately to the all-important surplus, which provided profits for policyholders and shareholders and was the real test of strength. Sometimes new business, with its heavy initial expenses, actually tended for a while to reduce the surplus. The vital balancing factor was the growth of investment income.

It was apparent by the late nineties that this growth was lagging. Mortgages, municipal bonds, and real estate, marked out by law and favoured by policy as the principal fields of investment, were delivering a yield that was adequate to support present volume. But they were not building for the future. Municipal bonds offered a set, unvarying return with little or no prospect of an increase in market value. Nor were they always quite so safe as they seemed. The risks of growth and change affected small towns and municipalities as well as industry itself, and there was sometimes delay or default in the payment of interest. Real estate holdings, subject to the same difficulties, appreciated only erratically if at all. Mortgages, usually short-term and on small properties, were expensive to obtain and service and posed the recurring problem of reinvestment. With a host of small transactions, administration was costly and returns were further reduced. The company's funds, employed in the ways of the nineties, were not keeping pace with the work of its men in the field. While the volume of incoming business drove it on, the slow growth of the surplus threatened to hold it back.

To all this, the Dominion Insurance Act of 1899 had added a new difficulty. Prior to that time the required legal reserve against policy liabilities had been established on the basis of a valuation of 4½ per cent. In other words, companies were allowed to assume that the average return on their invested assets would be at that rate. From 1894 Sun Life had bettered this by calculating its own reserve on a return of 4 per cent. With the passing of the new act, however, all companies were required to set up reserves at a basis of 3½ per cent on policies issued after January 1, 1900, while the reserves of prior policies would have to be calculated on the 4-per-cent basis by 1910 and on the 3½-per-cent basis by 1915. To the Macaulays, the requirement was excessive and was likely to drive the smaller companies to the wall. In the case of Sun Life, having protested the new provision they prepared to carry it out. They were to succeed so well that by 1905, ten years ahead of the required time, all the company's policies would be established on the new basis. As of January 1, 1900, however, the one glaring certainty was that over a million dollars would have to be accumulated as an additional reserve against policies then in force.

NEW INVESTMENT FIELDS

Fortunately for the company, the cloud blown over from Ottawa had been equipped with a silver lining. The new act, in its investment provisions, recognized the changing needs of the twentieth century. To the old narrow fields that had been open to insurance companies, the fields of industrial bonds and approved public services were now added. Capital could go where capital was in clamorous demand and could gain a high return still consistent with safety. The funds that had been comparatively static could now be channelled into the thousands of expanding industries, the railway and street-car and inter-urban transit lines, and the processes of growth and electrification that were changing the face of the continent. It was a move exactly in keeping with the Macaulays' assessment of the times, and they were not slow to act on it.

As the law came into effect Sun Life began to acquire its first small holdings under the new dispensation. Late in 1902, T. B. Macaulay was authorized to investigate the possibilities of large-scale investment in the field of public utilities. His search led him southwest to Illinois and the complex of towns and cities in the central area where gas companies, electric light companies, street railways, and inter-urban services were thriving on the rich black soil of the Corn Belt and the wealth of the mines beneath it. There was no question here either of the need of capital or the certainty of growth, and Sun Life began its purchases of blocks of the best bonds. They were to coalesce as they grew under the wings of the Illinois Traction Company, a holding company, which rapidly extended its interests to the control and operation of fifty-five subsidiaries in Illinois, Missouri, Iowa, Kansas, and Nebraska. Twenty years later, when Sun Life disposed of its holdings, this first great series of public utility investments was to be concluded, without the loss of a day's interest or default on a single bond, by the handing over of a cheque in favour of Sun Life for $30,903,881.17. It was admired at the time as the largest cheque ever drawn in favour of a Canadian corporation. Much of it represented profit, and all of it was reinvested on the same day received.

The new investment policy marked the turning of an important corner. Within five years of its inception, the worries about the surplus had been replaced by pride in its growth. In 1908, with the volume of new business increasing annually by about 15 per cent, Sun Life passed its old friend and rival, Canada Life, to become the leading Canadian company in business in force. At the same period, however, with all Canadian companies, it was involved in new anxieties.

INVESTIGATION AND LEGISLATION

The development of life insurance in the United States had been enormous, exuberant, and subject to some abuses. In 1905 a commission of investigation in the state of New York, under Senator William W. Armstrong, established among other facts that government supervision had been lax and sometimes corrupt. There had been corrupt directors and officials in some companies; there had been cases of bad management and bad investment practices. The inevitable result, when the findings of the commission were revealed, was hostile public opinion and stringent legislation.

Some features of the so-called Armstrong Law, which followed the Armstrong commission, were good and necessary. Robertson Macaulay's stand of years before was vindicated by a recommendation that officers and directors should be prohibited from any personal interest in the financial transactions of the company. It was required, in accordance with Sun's practice since 1895, that the standard guarantees be published in the policy itself. Yet much of the law, to a knowledgeable insurance man, was an unrelieved nightmare. By the middle of 1907 this 'national catastrophe', as T. B. Macaulay called it, had reduced the volume of insurance in American companies by $500 million.

From the restrictive legislation of New York State, Sun Life was mercifully free, as it did not do business there. The stir to the south, however, was soon reflected in the north, and the cry rose in Canada for a similar investigation. On February 28, 1906, a Royal Commission was established, and the investigation that followed was thorough, trying, and protracted. Every detail in the practice of Canadian companies was required to be laid bare, and insurance executives were subjected to intensive examination. The influence of the Armstrong findings in the United States was still strong, and it was the first business of Sun Life, in common with other companies, to show that Canada was free of abuses. For that work, and for the conduct of business in the future, the Macaulay prescription was simple. 'Let the public know just what a company does . . . if the business has to be conducted in the limelight there will be few evils.'

It was an attitude based on confidence, and it was borne out by the results. Minor defects in practice came in for some criticism, but Canadian companies as a whole emerged with a clean bill of health. Legislators desired, and were now prepared to believe that the companies also desired, the best protection for policyholders on the soundest business principles. A new act, when it was passed in 1910, fulfilled most of the hopes. Government powers were extended and clarified. The technical provisions were practical and realistic, while the investment powers of the act of 1899 were maintained and even widened.

Once again, in the new Dominion Insurance Act, some of the practices of Sun Life were incorporated and given the force of law. At one point it had been suggested that since the policyholders of a company represented the great bulk of its resources, they should also be represented on the Board of Directors. 'I can only say,' rejoined T. B. Macaulay to this, 'that as soon as we see any sign whatever of a desire on the part of the policyholders to have a vote, then we will certainly take it into serious consideration.'

The board took action on the matter prior to the annual meeting in 1911. The number of directors was increased from nine to twelve, with the provision that four of these should represent policyholders. The Honourable Raoul Dandurand, W. M. Birks, C. R. Hosmer, and H. Warren K. Hale were the first men so elected.

REINSURANCE
THE FIELD FORCE
THE MACAULAY CLUB

As the company's growth continued in other directions, bulk reinsurance rose to a new importance. In 1910 Sun Life acquired the $4.6 million business of the Royal-Victoria Life Insurance Company of Canada, and in 1913 that of the Home Life Association of Canada, totalling $5.1 million. In 1914 a special department was established for reinsurance, and in the next year the $28 million business of The Federal Life Insurance Company of Canada as well as the $1.3 million participating business of The Security Life Insurance Company of Canada was taken over.

Meanwhile, the work of the men in the field was a constant preoccupation. With the Macaulays it came first, whatever their other concerns. By the turn of the century they had passed through the first easy-going, rather haphazard period of development in which general agents, responsible for a defined territory, had built up their own field forces on their own terms of employment. They had come to the conclusion that every agent of Sun Life should be approved and hired directly by the company. The general agent would become the salaried manager of a territory, his men would still report to him, but a common basic principle would govern their remuneration. They would be assured, through a direct contract with Sun Life, first of a fair immediate return on sales and secondly of a scale of additional allowances which would sustain their continuing interest in business already secured.

By the early years of the century these principles, with occasional modifications, governed the Sun's relations with its agents. Results and morale alike testified to their general acceptance. Frederick G. Cope, who had joined the company in 1889 and become Superintendent of Agencies, played a large part in introducing the changes and in solving the attendant problems. T. B. Macaulay, always fertile in ideas, possessed the knack of stimulating ideas in others. Out of the Agency Outing in 1902 came the idea for the *Agency Bulletin,* later to grow to *The Monthly Agency Review.* On the way to that, however, at the Outing of 1910, it struck off another thought. From the agents gathered for that year came the suggestion of a company club which would embrace the leaders in the field and be open to all agents as they reached an annual production of $100,000. The advantages and incentives were obvious, and there was one choice for the name. The Macaulay Club was formed, honouring Robertson Macaulay, and the long roll of its membership continues to grow with the company.

TO THE FIRST WORLD WAR

In the period between 1900 and the First World War the work in the foreign field was mainly of consolidation. In 1905 the growth of the business in India was attested to by the completion by the company of the fine new Canada Building in Bombay. In 1913, with the opening of an office at Cape Town, Sun Life made its long-delayed advance into South Africa. Balancing these, however, were withdrawals from other fields. The agencies in France and Holland were closed out in 1906 and the agency in Belgium in 1912.

In Montreal, on May 13, 1914, Robertson Macaulay laid the cornerstone of the new Head Office building of Sun Life. A site, facing on Dominion Square, had been chosen in 1908, and in 1914 the company owned not only the former property of the Y.M.C.A. but also the adjoining property of Knox Church, which was to be left in the possession of the church for another four years. The initial building, designed to provide accommodation for 750 clerks, was to occupy only the first portion of this site, extending for about two-thirds of the distance between Metcalfe and Mansfield streets. Its design had begun in 1912, and was to be the last absorbing interest of Robertson Macaulay's life.

He was not to see the completion of the massively graceful structure, with its six fluted Corinthian columns facing Dominion Square and its general impression of strong and simple dignity. He had come to the laying of the cornerstone, a man of eighty-one, convalescing unsurely from a serious operation. For more than a year afterward his health seemed to return, and there was scarcely any abatement of his usual activity. On September 27, 1915, however, following a chill that developed into pneumonia, the end came.

He was saluted around the world by the men of an insurance world that he had done much to change. In his own company his death marked the closing of an era and the opening of another. Alexander Walker Ogilvie had preceded him by thirteen years, dying in 1902 as his fast friend and supporter. He himself in 1908, as he brought the company to the head of the Canadian field, had performed an act of partial abdication. The directors at that time had voted him an increase in salary. He had declined it 'in view of his advancing years'. His son, the Secretary, he said, 'has been carrying, and carrying successfully, the burden of the strenuous management of the company' and might wear better than he the title of Managing Director. That change had been made, T. B. Macaulay had become Secretary and Managing Director; but his father had remained President and the influence of Robertson Macaulay had been felt in the company's affairs to the last day of his life.

Now that was ended and the full burden of management descended on other men. On October 5, 1915, T. B. Macaulay became President and Managing Director, with F. G. Cope succeeding as Secretary. Samuel H. Ewing, who had succeeded Alexander Walker Ogilvie, remained as Vice-President. Arthur Barton Wood, who had been appointed Actuary on the day that T. B. Macaulay became Managing Director, continued in that post. E. A. Macnutt, who had come to the investment department in 1904, retained the position of Treasurer which he had held since 1906.

The annual statement of Sun Life for 1915 showed a total of nearly $35 million of new insurance written, as compared to the $10.5 million of 1900. Insurance in force had increased nearly five times over, to $257 million; and total assets more than seven times over, to $74 million. The $423,000 which had been the surplus in 1900 had grown to $7.5 million. The position of the company was impregnable by the measuring sticks of the past. But the past was done with. Canada was in the midst of a great war, and it was a war like no other. One could feel already the tremors of mighty change, rippling under the carnage, widening across the earth. The old was tumbling in wreckage, and it would be a new world after the peace. It must be thought of and prepared for, but meanwhile the war came first.

7

'High Noon'

THE WAR YEARS

Four months before the death of Robertson Macaulay one of the oldest traditions of the company came to an end. On May 11, 1915, the directors changed the rule under which, for forty-four years, the board had met weekly. Henceforth the full meetings would be held only once a month, but within that framework a delegation of functions was to provide for closer control. One standing committee of the board was to deal solely with investments. A second, similar committee was to deal with 'questions arising out of the general business of the company apart from investments'. Each committee, while reporting to the board monthly, would meet whenever required by the work in its own field and would maintain a constant review of its own problems. Sun Life, with the volume and complexity of normal business increasing and the strain of the war added, was embarked on a long process that would soon grow and ramify. There would be more such subdivision as time went on. More and more there would be separately expanding departments requiring specialized attention, yet the linked operations must be kept in a smooth flow. The streamlined committee system that would extend down through the company was taking shape at the top.

In all departments of Sun Life, through the four years of war, there was change and adaptation and sometimes improvisation. The investment policy that had been wholly concerned with advancing the growth of profits became part of the war effort. Interest rates, which were steadily climbing in the industrial field, became a secondary consideration. The funds of Sun Life, and of other insurance companies, were one of the great sources of the nation's financial strength, and they were made available to the full extent required. In the launching of the Canadian war loans and Victory Loans Sun Life was an adviser to the government as well as a principal subscriber, and its field force were as active in the bond campaigns as they were in the selling of insurance. The company was a large subscriber to the war loans of Great Britain and other allied governments. By the war's end Sun Life's total purchases of all the various issues had reached nearly $50 million, and earnings had suffered in consequence. Mortality rates had been higher during the war, and the effects of the great influenza epidemic of 1918 had been almost as serious. Yet the company, like the country itself, came out of the long ordeal with a new strength and confidence.

Forty-two men, almost half the male staff at Head Office in August 1914, had gone into the services. One hundred and twenty-eight had gone from the branch offices and field force. The company had carried on with older or unfit men, with women hastily recruited, and with a few returning casualties in the later years of the war. Of its men in the services, by the war's end eleven had been killed and twenty-five wounded. Those who came back had missed up to four full years of precious business experience. They had to cope with change, they had to cope with the restlessness of war and they had to cope, more pleasantly, with the new status of women. In 1914 they had left about a hundred girls behind them at the desks in Head Office. In May 1919 there were 250 women to 150 men. Yet there was a bond of mutual respect between those who had fought the war and those who had worked at home, and it eased every transition. On both sides there was gratitude to the tired senior men who had struggled with green help and depleted agency staffs and had somehow kept the business moving forward.

The returning soldier, sailor, or airman had had the difference between his service pay and his company salary made up to him through all his time in the forces. He had retained his seniority and was already receiving the benefit of a cost-of-living bonus. There was now a non-contributory pension plan, established in 1917, as well as the plan of life insurance, existing since 1910, on which the company paid half the premium. There were, in addition, the ample and gracious surroundings of the new Head Office building on Dominion Square, into which the company had moved in March 1918. All in all, for most of the Sun Life men who had gone to war, it seemed good to be back.

REBUILDING AND REORGANIZATION

They and the company were now entering upon a decade of many changes and of hugely expanded growth. The processes of industrialization and urbanization, vastly accelerated by the war, were transforming North America. For hundreds of thousands of families, as they moved in to the cities from farms and small towns, the weekly pay of the bread winner became the sole means of subsistence. The importance of his life and health rose in proportion and so did the demand for insurance. In the higher echelons of industry the growth of large corporations and the increasing weight of taxes brought the need for new protection. It was seen that life insurance could provide against death duties and inheritance taxes, against the loss of key executives, the breaking up of partnerships, and the many drastic changes that death might bring. Yet above all and transcending all were the effects of the war itself. The dreadful totals of the casualty lists, and the almost equally dreadful totals of the deaths from influenza in the epidemic of 1918, seemed to have impressed people anew with their frail grip on life. There was a new desire for security, a new urge to protect and be protected; and this, with the other factors, combined in a demand for life insurance that had never been known before.

The company was well aware of the new conditions, and it moved swiftly to meet them. A first need was staff. From the early twenties onward, in the Head Office, in the branch offices, and in the field, the acquisition and training of suitable men was a major preoccupation. At the same time, by means of aptitude tests, study courses, and a search through the universities for promising graduates, standards were forced upward. Edward E. Duckworth, a former member of the actuarial department as well as a former schoolmaster, became Assistant Secretary in charge of personnel, and in all his selection methods he was guided by the President's dictum. 'I have laid it down as a rule,' said T. B. Macaulay, 'that we must not knowingly engage any man on our clerical force who does not have sufficient education and ability to make him likely to rise to the position of a chief clerk.'

In the field the basic principles of the company's organization remained unchanged. Branch managers, as the representatives of Head Office in the territory assigned to them, retained the sole responsibility of building a sales force and assisting and training agents. But their work was powerfully supplemented in 1921 by the establishment of a Field Service Bureau, directed from Head Office and ranging through all the territories with the function of informing agents on the company's practices, developing instructional literature, and dealing with special problems. Again in 1923, as a further measure of control and co-ordination, James C. Tory became chairman of an Agency Executive Committee which included agency superintendents and supervisors and of which the President and Vice-President were ex-officio members.

LIFE INSURANCE: ITS WIDENING RESPONSIBILITIES AND CAPABILITIES

In all its development through this first post-war decade the company was responding to the new attitude of the public. It meant to profit by the demand for life insurance, it meant to grow in Canada and abroad, and it meant to advance in the United States. But with the promise of growth came new responsibilities and a widening of its own attitude. It became apparent to Sun Life, and not to the Sun alone but to all insurance companies, that the improvement of public health was a joint interest of the insurer and the insured. Sun Life, therefore, became with the other companies a large contributor to the work of medical research. It became interested in special areas where special diseases were prevalent, and some of its work in this field was done very close to home. In Montreal, during the typhoid epidemic of 1927, Sun Life through its medical bureau set up free clinics at which some fifty thousand people received inoculations. More generally, throughout the whole scope of the company's business and by means of a wide range of educational activities, Sun Life sought not only to teach people but to learn from them. 'We have shifted our ground,' said George H. Harris, supervisor of the Field Service Bureau. 'We are not so much today seeking to sell our policies as we are searching for the reasons why people should buy them.'

The search was directed also towards a widening and modernization of the field of insurance protection. Since 1910, the first year permitted by law, the company had had a clause in its policies providing a waiver of premiums in cases of total and permanent disability. In 1918, with the door opened by a new amendment to the Dominion Insurance Act, it moved further. In addition to the waiver of his premiums and without reduction of his insurance, a policyholder of Sun Life who became totally and permanently disabled could now receive an annual income of 10 per cent of the face value of his policy. By 1922, when this annual income was increased to 1 per cent monthly, the company was also offering a double indemnity provision in case of death by accident.

The offering of life insurance without medical examination was another important development in 1922. Many companies had studied the subject and as early as 1880 Robertson Macaulay had made the first tentative experiments for the Sun when he accepted a few policies for Hudson's Bay Company factors in the remote North West Territories. Though his efforts had come to little, the line of his thinking remained, gradually impressing itself on the actuaries of many companies. Not only in the wilderness but in towns and cities as well, it was very often difficult to get a prospect to a doctor or a doctor to a prospect. People were often discouraged from taking out policies by the mere inconvenience or their mere dislike of a medical examination. It was usually possible, moreover, to obtain much of the necessary information through other forms of inquiry. By 1921 the Confederation Life Association began to accept small non-medical risks as it satisfied itself of the force of the various arguments. On May 5, 1922, Sun Life announced its plan. Within definite age limits and on risks which began at a maximum of $2,000 and were gradually increased to $10,000 and in later years to substantially higher amounts, it would accept policies without medical examination.

With this advance and with the steady improvement of the

system for rating under-average lives, the protection of life insurance was extended to new hundreds of thousands. Yet the greatest advance of the decade was in the field of group life insurance. It was a development keyed to the expansion of corporations and the growth of great industries, and it had been held back in Canada only by an interpretation of insurance law. During the war, though companies had already begun to feel the need of blanket protection for large numbers of employees, the Federal Superintendent of Insurance had ruled that this was not permissible under the Insurance Act. By late 1919, however, as the need grew and the pressure mounted, the act was re-studied and the superintendent changed his position. Within two months Sun Life wrote its first policy of group life insurance covering the employees of a large mid-western newspaper organization. Sun Life was the first Canadian company to enter the new field, and within seven years it was writing group life insurance in Canada, the United States, and Great Britain at the rate of $35 million annually.

In the same period, as the forms of protection widened, the assistance to beneficiaries continued to grow. A lump sum, paid over to a named recipient on the death of a policyholder, ended the company's formal obligation. But it very often failed of its basic purpose, which was the protection of wives and children who knew little about handling money. With that in mind, the company had long since introduced a system of settlement options by which the beneficiary of a policyholder could, if desired, leave all or any part of a death claim on deposit with Sun Life. It would earn immediately the same rate of interest that was paid to living policyholders and it would participate in the future profits of the company. By 1926 the rate of interest was 5½ per cent, and at the end of that year the scale on which it was based was still further increased.

BULK AND SURPLUS REINSURANCE

Sun Life had responded to the new opportunities and was reaping the full rewards. In every field of the business improved organization, improved methods and training, and improved plans of protection were resulting in huge increases in annual volume. They came from Canada and from the United States and abroad, and they were everywhere powerfully supported by another facet of growth.

The acquisition of bulk reinsurance had continued throughout the war and expanded with the coming of peace. The business of The Prudential Life Insurance Company, a Canadian company, was taken over in 1916, and that of The British Columbia Life Assurance Company in 1917. In 1918-19 the business of the Provincial Life Insurance Company was acquired, and in 1924 Sun Life came to the rescue of the Northwestern Life Assurance Company of Winnipeg, reinsuring its total business, and bringing the Canadian reinsurances acquired by the company to a total of $58.5 million.

In 1923, large transactions in the Far East brought the company $42 million of reinsurance from the taking-over of The Shanghai Life Insurance Company Limited and The China Mutual Life Insurance Company Limited, two associated concerns. Of even more importance in the field of foreign business were the gradual effects of the Armstrong Law in New York State. A provision of that law had limited all companies to a specific, graduated amount of new business annually, and many of the companies could obtain the permitted amount in the United States alone. They therefore decided to curtail their business abroad. With the abandonment of new underwritings went the need for foreign agencies, and Sun Life with its widespread network became a natural beneficiary. Mutual of New York reinsured with Sun Life its entire British business. This transaction, in 1923, was only part of a long withdrawal from foreign fields in which the New York Life and the Equitable of New York also participated, bringing to Sun Life eventually a total in reinsurances of some $134 million.

In 1926 Sun Life, which had only recently established an office in Cleveland, Ohio, took over the business of the Cleveland Life Insurance Company, amounting to $36 million. It was the first occasion on which a Canadian company had absorbed an American life insurance company, and it was followed two years later by an even larger transaction. On January 1, 1928, Sun Life acquired the business of the Western Union Life Insurance Company of Spokane, Washington, amounting to $87 million. On each occasion Sun Life's advance into the field of American life insurance was given a new impetus by the acquiring of a trained organization. Valuable new staff, in addition to the new business, had also come with the acquisitions in Canada and abroad. In all cases, to policyholders, they represented a gain. Every policy reinsured was guaranteed in its entirety.

Another class of business developed from 1922, stimulated by an increasing demand for large policies to meet succession duties and other forms of taxation. Sun Life up to that time had not given much thought to surplus reinsurance, which is the amount over the maximum that any company wishes to carry on a single life. It became advisable, however, as policies were being requested in excess of the company's then maximum of $100,000; and it was decided in certain cases not only to place reinsurance but to accept it from other companies. The first large acquisition of surplus reinsurance came on July 1, 1924, from the First Reinsurance Company of Hartford. It amounted to $30.5 million, and it only signalled the opening of another avenue of growth. By 1927 Sun Life's total of surplus reinsurances, acquired from over seventy companies, amounted to $142 million.

INVESTMENT IN COMMON STOCKS

Supporting all this growth was the company's investment policy, which had evolved once more in response to changing conditions. By the end of 1927, 55 per cent of the assets of Sun Life were represented by public utility, railroad, and industrial securities, and of that total considerably more than half was in common stocks. T. B. Macaulay, who had hailed the coming of one great era of development at the turn of the century, had sensed the coming of another with the end of the war. He was resolved that the company should share in and be a part of it. Industrialization, he felt, was to be the keynote of the new age, and participation in industry would be the cornerstone of investment policy.

To his mind there could be full participation only through the purchase of common stocks, which represented a true and actual share in the ownership of great companies. Selection was all-important but he was guided in that, not only by the provisions of the Dominion Insurance Act, but by the lines of his own policy, which went a great deal further. From 1923 onward, as Sun Life expanded its investment department and developed its investment practice, stringent rules had been laid down. First of all, Sun Life must be thoroughly familiar with the operations, the directing personnel, and the management practices of any company in which it proposed to invest. Stocks would be purchased only in corporations which had had a long and successful career and which provided basically the necessities or conveniences of life. Large reserves must have been accumulated and heavy provision made against depreciation and possible contingencies, and the company must be dominant in its field. No common stock, moreover, was to be purchased for early sale or for the purpose of making an immediate profit. 'In making our selections,' said Macaulay, 'we always have in mind the distant future. We are extremely cautious and conservative in making our selections; once we have bought, however, we retain our holdings indefinitely, regardless of market fluctuations . . . looking for our profit not on the stock exchange but in the steady growth and gradually increasing prosperity of the corporation.'

With these principles established, Sun Life under Thomas Bassett Macaulay had set itself to participate in the growth of the industrial life of North America. It had remained at the same time firmly aware of its own special function. It would have no part in the management of any corporation and would hold no more than 10 per cent of the stock. 'We are investors and only investors,' Macaulay said. 'We have enlisted many large groups of the brainiest, most experienced, most energetic, and most successful men on the continent to work for us and maintain our interest earnings.' It was a policy that would come in question a few years later when these men, like all men and nations, were in the grip of the great depression; yet it would be justified in the long future. It seemed beyond doubt or question at the time he spoke. In 1927, through a period of declining interest rates, Sun Life's rate of return on its invested assets had risen steadily, and for the seventh successive year it had increased the scale of dividends payable to policyholders.

'WE SET OUR OWN PACE'

In January 1924 the Sun Life *Agency Review* had reported that 'In order to better adapt our Montreal organization to the service of the public an additional division office has been established which will be known as Montreal Uptown Division.' It was the first of the multiple branches which the company was later to establish in many cities throughout its sphere of operations. By 1927, to its twenty-four branch offices in Canada, the company had added thirty-two in the United States, serving twenty-eight states, the District of Columbia, and Hawaii. Twenty-one branches were operating in the British Isles, while thirty-two additional branch and district offices extended the business almost around the world. Total assets, at the end of 1927, had risen to over $400 million and the surplus to $45 million, while insurance in force, which had passed the billion-dollar mark in 1925, was now nearly $1.5 billion. It was the fruit of a great era for all life insurance companies, crowning a quarter-century in which the volume of insurance in force in North America had multiplied nearly ten times over. But Sun Life's progress had been in a class by itself. In 1927 alone, where the new business of American companies had increased by about 1 per cent and the new business of Canadian companies by about 7 per cent, Sun Life's rate of increase had been 23 per cent. 'We,' said T. B. Macaulay, 'set our own pace.'

BUILDINGS AND STAFF

In London, in 1922, the company had purchased the beautiful home of John Jacob Astor, one of the most exquisite houses in the British Empire, for use as its British Department headquarters. Within five years, however, the premises had become too small, and on July 1, 1927, T. B. Macaulay had laid the cornerstone of an imposing new building. It was rising on Cockspur Street with a frontage on Pall Mall, and would become a permanent addition to the skyline of Trafalgar Square.

In Montreal the Head Office building occupied in 1918 had been very quickly outgrown. By 1923 a new section was rising on the old site of Knox Church, and by 1926 it was a part of the original structure, extending the building from Metcalfe Street to Mansfield Street. Yet even as this was completed to house a staff which had grown to almost fifteen hundred, there were other plans in train. Designs were being prepared, to be executed in stages, both for a northward extension of the building and for a tower which would rise to a height of twenty-six storeys. The whole, when completed, would be the tallest as well as one of the finest buildings in the British Empire, and would ultimately provide for a staff of between ten and twelve thousand.

It would never house such numbers as employees of Sun Life. The first crude calculators were already heralding the day when machines would do the work of many hands. For the staff of that day, however, to whom the world of computers and automation was yet unknown, all things seemed possible. Morale was high, and a post with Sun Life meant much to the friends outside. 'They used to look at us and envy us,' records one veteran of those days. Macaulay loved to speak of the company as a family, and though he could no longer follow his old custom of meeting and chatting with each new employee, there was much to justify the word. There were the Sun Life recreation clubs and sports clubs, the football, billiards, bowling, and cricket teams, the choral groups and theatrical and minstrel troupes, and there was the Sun Life cafeteria in the building where everyone was provided with a good lunch at the company's expense. Standing out above all, perhaps, were the annual staff outings at Mount Victoria, T. B. Macaulay's country home near Hudson, Quebec. Each year on the day appointed, a special train carried the hundreds of Sun Life men and women to the station at Hudson Heights, where they were met by gaily decorated cars and haycarts and always by their beaming host. From there it was off to the picnic and the games and to a general running about among the fine Shetland ponies, the prize Holsteins, and the choice crops of what was described as one of the finest experimental farms in the Dominion.

As always, the years had brought their changes in the senior ranks. In 1923 both Samuel H. Ewing and Frederick G. Cope had died, the one to be succeeded as Vice-President by Arthur B. Wood, and the other as Secretary by H. Warren K. Hale. Another loss, where regret was tempered with pleasure, came on January 31, 1926, when James C. Tory resigned as General Manager of Agencies. He had resigned after accepting an appointment as Lieutenant-Governor of Nova Scotia, and he was elected a director of Sun Life when he ceased to be an officer. Also in 1926, Sir Phiroze C. Sethna became General Manager for India. The scion of a notable Indian family, prominent in the industrial life and public affairs of the country, Sethna had commenced with Sun Life as Resident Secretary at Bombay in 1901, and had been Manager for India, Burma, and Ceylon since 1920. Already widely travelled and internationally known, he was to continue to be a force in the company up to his retirement in 1933.

T.B.M.'s FIFTIETH ANNIVERSARY

Among many changes, however, the presidency remained unchanged. For the staff now it was in the very nature of things to have a Macaulay at the head of the company, and few among them remembered anyone but T.B. He had come to seem as permanent as those always-rising figures in the annual statements, as the rising Sun itself. Certainly he had done much to promote that rise. A Fellow of the Institute of Actuaries (Great Britain) and of the Actuarial Society of America, he had served twice as president of the society and once as president of The Canadian Life Insurance Officers Association. On the technical side of his profession he had helped to make life insurance a vastly better and more useful servant of humanity. He had made Sun Life one of the great companies of the world. It surprised no one else, if it surprised him, when he walked in on Monday, October 3, 1927, to find his office crowded with flowers and his desk heaped high with letters and telegrams of congratulation from the staffs and agencies of the company and from high insurance executives around the world.

Sunday, the day before, had been the fiftieth anniversary of the day he joined Sun Life. At the Windsor Hotel later there was a large banquet and a company dance in his honour, and the speeches of many notables might well have been suffocating if they had not been so warmly offered and so firmly based on truth. It was in the same spirit that, on October 5, 1927, the Board of Directors decided that an historical record of the company be prepared and dedicated to T. B. Macaulay under the title of *The President's Book.* Written by George H. Harris, and published in 1928, the volume remains to this day not only lively and readable, but a priceless source of information from which much of the early material for the present sketch has been drawn. There were many other gifts for the President, of which one charmed him in particular. It was a handsome grandfather's clock that came to him from the field officers with the hope that he might have many years to listen to the sweet chimes. 'We pledge you our word,' said the man who made the presentation, 'that if earnestness and determination count for anything it will always be "high noon" with the Sun Life of Canada.'

8

'We have hitched our investment policy to the star of this continent'

FIRST TREMORS

In October 1929, as the great stock market panics heralded the coming of the great depression, T. B. Macaulay was entering his seventieth year. He had been as forehanded as any man in preparing for what might come, and he was to find like all others that he had not prepared enough. Yet he spoke with his old confidence, and he spoke for a longer future, as the company girded itself to meet the thirties. Some 52 per cent of the assets of Sun Life were now invested in the common stocks of companies and corporations, mainly in North America and dependent on North America. He made no apologies for that. 'We believe,' he said at the annual meeting on February 11, 1930, 'in the future of Montreal, of New York, of Chicago . . . we believe even more in the future of our entire nations – both Canada and the United States. We have hitched our investment policy to the star of this continent, and in particular to our great cities, and just as surely as they continue to grow and prosper, so surely will our investments grow and prosper.'

He had much to support his confidence at the time he spoke. So far as the stock market was concerned, he had been well aware of its hugely inflated values and had made provision against them. 'Our policy,' he said, 'is so to undervalue our holdings that there can be a tremendous drop in prices without ever reaching the figures at which our securities are carried in our accounts.' He had pointed out a year before that market quotations on the company's holdings could shrink by as much as a hundred million dollars without reducing the surplus by one dollar. That statement had been tested and had held good. Not only had the company absorbed the shock of the October crashes without visible weakening of its position; it had gone on in spite of them to the greatest year in its history. By December 31, 1929, though security holdings were still carried at values far below the market, assets and reserves had both shown large increases and the surplus had grown to $60 million.

He could point to more than that. In the two years since his jubilee, as in all the years of his presidency, every department of the business had reflected enormous growth. Insurance in force stood now at $2.4 billion. The company, with its business still expanding in Great Britain, India, the Orient, and the old fields abroad, was now also operating in thirty-seven of the American states. In Canada it was pre-eminent, and it had everywhere become proverbial for the treatment accorded policyholders. Since 1910 the holders of participating policies had been entitled by law to a minimum of 90 per cent of the distributable profits. For thirty-two years they had been receiving 95 per cent. In 1929, for the ninth successive year, dividend scales had been increased. Also on January 1, 1929, a special maturity dividend had become effective which would further increase benefits. This dividend, originally for matured participating policies which had been ten years in force, was in 1930 applicable to policies held for five years or more, and would range upward on the basis of current earnings from a minimum of 5 per cent to a maximum of 15 per cent of the face value of the policy. The President could say with justice that 'in profitableness to our policyholders we are not excelled by any life company in the world'.

THE ONSET OF DEPRESSION

All this had been supported and made possible by investments hitched to the star of North America. Yet there was a harsh corollary which was soon to become apparent. The wagon hitched to the star must follow the star, and for North America now the course was downward. The stock market panics had been only a first symptom of the vast, world-wide sickness which was to disrupt trade, destroy confidence, and bring the economies of nations to the verge of collapse. For almost four years, as great industries stood paralysed, factory gates closed and millions walked the streets in search of jobs, the very base of investment seemed to dissolve. For Thomas Bassett Macaulay the high noon of the twenties faded to a bleak twilight, and he was not to see the end of it as President of Sun Life.

On December 6, 1967, Alistair M. Campbell, as President of the company, delivered an assessment of Macaulay in an address to The Newcomen Society in North America. He recognized in the former president the qualities once ascribed to him by an earlier writer: 'a spaciousness, an adequacy, and a fearlessness that bespeaks at once the man of thought and the man of action'. Macaulay, he went on, had been a firm believer in common stocks as an investment for life insurance companies. 'In this he stood alone amongst the leaders of insurance companies in North America, though he had some measure of support in the practices of some British insurance companies. He was not alone in his views in the company, for the founders had set the precedent by buying stocks of banks even in the company's first year of business. The wisdom of a life insurance company investing a portion of its funds in common stocks is today generally accepted. T. B. Macaulay's thinking was far ahead of his time. The stocks were selected with care and in the longer term they have enhanced the fortunes of the company. In his enthusiasm, however, T. B. Macaulay committed too large a proportion of the company's funds to common stocks. When the depression came, a temporary cloud was set over a great man.' The growth he had hoped for would come – in the end he would be borne out – but he had neglected the nearer pitfalls and they were to prove dangerously deep.

So far as the business of Sun Life was concerned, its actual volume of underwritings did not commence to decline until 1931. Even at the end of that year its total of insurance in force, still rising, had passed $3 billion. Towards the end of 1930 it had made headline news in the insurance world by securing a group policy covering the employees of the huge Illinois Central Railroad System. This policy, the largest in the company's history to that time, provided benefits ranging to a maximum of $10,000 per person, together with health and accident indemnities. It was regarded throughout the industry as one of the most important life insurance transactions of the decade.

Nevertheless, by the close of 1931 the impact of general conditions had forced Sun Life to take stringent measures. With growth stopped everywhere, with great corporations passing their regular dividends, and with the best of gilt-edged securities almost unsaleable, stock market prices sagged below all reserves and became in fact meaningless. Executives of Sun Life as well as of other companies with equity holdings, in consultation with officials of the Dominion Government Insurance Department and with government insurance officials in the United States, had to go over their portfolios stock by stock and determine an official value. With these values as basis the annual statements appeared, and they were sadly changed from the past. The surplus of $60 million in 1929 became $31 million in 1930, $16 million in 1931, and by the end of 1932 it declined to less than $6 million, where it was to remain for three more years.

Meanwhile, and of equal importance to the life of the company, was the question of annual income. New insurance fell from a total of $705 million in 1930 to a total of $216 million in 1933. Renewal business faltered as hard-pressed policyholders failed to meet their premiums. Interest earned on assets declined from its high of 7.02 per cent in 1929 to a low of 4.06 per cent in 1934. At the same time, with unemployment gripping the continent and banks in the United States closing their doors, thousands of policyholders who had exhausted their other savings turned to life insurance. Through long months, while Sun Life itself was straitened for liquid assets, it was sending cash for policy loans to points in the United States and supplying the many borrowers who applied at Canadian offices. The annual outflow of new policy loans and surrender values climbed from $27 million in 1929 to $58 million in 1933, by which time the worst was past.

ATTACK, DEFENCE, AND RECOVERY

The real anxieties of the period might have seemed enough, but they were added to by a number of minor pinpricks. Of these the

The 'Canada Building' in Bombay, built by the Company and opened in 1905, was the headquarters of Sun Life operations in India, Burma, and Ceylon.

Macaulay Club agency conference near Boston in 1929.
(Photograph continued on following 6 pages.)

Robertson Macaulay, then 81, laying the cornerstone of the first portion of the present Head Office Building – May 13, 1914.

A multi-horse team delivers the 45-ton door frame for the new Head Office security vault on a snowy day in 1917.

The new Head Office Building, shortly after its opening in 1918.

Thomas Bassett Macaulay, third President, 1915-34.

The Head Office Building grows rapidly skyward – spring 1930.

King George VI and Queen Elizabeth pass the Sun Life Building on their triumphal tour of Canada – May 1939.

Head Office Building and Dominion Square, 1940.

sharpest and most aggravating was provided by J. J. Harpell, a publisher of several trade papers in Gardenvale, Quebec. A man of moderate success and considerable ability, Harpell had among his other attainments a smattering of actuarial science. A policyholder and early friend of Sun Life, he had applied in 1928 for a mortgage loan, and had been declined. Another company had accepted the mortgage and there was no evidence that he was particularly resentful, but he had certainly turned from then on to a close and hostile study of the company's affairs. By 1929 he was convinced that it was badly managed and by 1930 T. B. Macaulay appeared to have become for him the embodiment of all crookedness.

His statistics and conclusions were published regularly in the *Journal of Commerce,* which was his own paper. They were further supported by the Policyholders' Association, which he had formed. Since the circulation of the paper was unaudited and very small and membership in the Policyholders' Association was limited to about a hundred of whom most were his own employees, it seemed unnecessary for a while to take his allegations very seriously. They were almost unanswerable in any case, since he found in the Sun Life balance sheet only what he wanted and surmised what he did not find. By 1932, however, Macaulay had had enough.

He had been accused personally of selling large blocks of his Sun Life stock at enormously inflated profits, and he had not silenced Harpell by showing that in thirty years he had disposed of exactly fifteen shares as a gift to a friend. He had been faced with a maze of technical charges on the company's profits, its dividend policies, its calculation of mortality rates and its settlement of claims, and as each wild inaccuracy was pinned down another had risen up. Harpell at first had been merely a sad joke to knowledgeable insurance men and members of the financial community, but few of them were any longer in the mood to laugh. On December 19, 1932, Harpell appeared before a judge and jury in the Court of King's Bench, Montreal, charged with criminal libel.

On December 23 the jury found him guilty. On December 27 the Honourable Chief Justice R. A. E. Greenshields, in sentencing him to three months in jail, declared flatly that 'you absolutely failed in one scintilla of proof'. On August 21, 1933, with his appeal dismissed and his sentence partially served, Harpell appeared before judicial authorities in Montreal to post a bond of two thousand dollars to keep the peace.

Meanwhile Sun Life went on, with hints by the end of 1933 of a return to better times. At the annual meeting of February 13, 1934, T. B. Macaulay announced that he was retiring as President of the company. There was great regret but there was not much surprise; he was a visibly aging man. There had to be too, and it was a tragic fact, a sense of relief at his going. Rightly or wrongly, he had come to represent for too many the too-great hopes and promises of an era that was now past. He was to be succeeded as President by Arthur Barton Wood, F.I.A., F.A.S., while E. A. Macnutt would become Vice-President and Treasurer. He himself was to be Chairman of the Board for a year, and later Chairman Emeritus. He would remain a director till his death in 1942, but he had addressed his last meeting and he would have no further hand in the shaping of policy. That would be, and had in fact already become, the work of younger men.

PRESIDENTS-TO-BE

The company, since the day T. B. Macaulay joined it in October 1877, had never had less than one future President somewhere at a desk in Head Office. It now had two. Alistair Matheson Campbell, a young Scot and a Master of Arts with first class honours in mathematics from the University of Aberdeen, had been recruited in 1928 and was already moving upward. George Wesley Bourke, who was now Actuary, had come up by the same long road that Campbell was now travelling. As a McGill student, he had worked two summers, 1915 and 1916, with the company and had decided on life insurance as a future career. Graduating in 1917 with the Anne Molson Gold Medal in Mathematics and Physics, he had joined the Canadian Garrison Artillery instead of Sun Life, and had returned from France in 1919 with the Military Medal and what promised to be a crippling wound. An almost useless right arm hung suspended in a sling and it was eyed rather dubiously by Arthur B. Wood, who was then Actuary, when the returning soldier walked in on him to claim a promised job. Bourke also intended to be an actuary, there was no doubt about that; but how would he handle a pen or a calculating machine and how would he survive the slim salaries and long years of bachelorhood that usually prefaced the career? The first answer was that he would become left-handed for a while, and there was no release for Wood from the promise he had made. Bourke got the job, married within a year against the strong advice of Wood, and proceeded not only to pass all his actuarial examinations but to recover the use of his arm after tedious years of treatment. Wood's scepticism as to the arm, the marriage, and the career had long since been dispelled and by the 1930s George W. Bourke, F.I.A., F.A.S., had become his right-hand man.

SENIOR PERSONNEL AND THE DIRECTORS

Under Wood, as he became President, there was a skilled senior staff, headed by Bourke, by E. A. Macnutt, and by C. S. V. Branch, who as Second Vice-President had devoted much of his attention to the matter of reinsurances. There was a powerful and widespread field force which had lost neither its loyalty nor its confidence in the face of hard times. In every department of the business there was long experience and confident expertise and there was also, supporting that, the power of renewal and change. Much of the resilience of the company came, as it always had, from a strong Board of Directors who were closely concerned with the business.

Almost every facet of industry and most aspects of the country's life were represented by the names on the board in 1933: Robert Adair, fuel merchant; E. W. Beatty of Canadian Pacific Railway; W. M. Birks of Henry Birks & Sons; the Honourable Raoul Dandurand, Montreal City & District Savings Bank; J. Redpath Dougall, publisher; Sir Herbert S. Holt, financier; J. W. McConnell of St. Lawrence Sugar Refineries; Ross H. McMaster, Steel Company of Canada; C. B. McNaught of British Empire Steel Corporation; Arthur B. Purvis, Canadian Industries Limited; Carl Riordon, paper manufacturer; John W. Ross, accountant; the Honourable L. A. Taschereau, lawyer and politician; the Honourable J. C. Tory, a former agency officer of the company; and the Honourable Lorne C. Webster, financier. There was allied here, in addition to strength and stability, a wide, far-ranging assortment of views and interests. They would make not only for sound management but for properly flexible management in the choosing of new directions.

ARTHUR B. WOOD

For all that was now required of him as the new head of the company, Arthur B. Wood was a man admirably equipped. He was known throughout the insurance fraternity of the world as an actuary of the highest professional qualifications. He was a Fellow of the Institute of Actuaries (Great Britain) and of the Actuarial Society of America. He had been a member of the council of the society and twice its president, and in 1923-4 had served as president of The Canadian Life Insurance Officers Association. Yet he had never allowed the technical side of the business to absorb the whole of his thinking. For two years, after the departure of James C. Tory in 1926, he had combined with the duties of Actuary the duties of chairman of the Agency Executive Committee, and he had gained in the process a thorough acquaintance and sympathy with the men at work in the field. Cool and knowledgeable, he had a warmly human side which was perhaps reflected as much by the priorities as by the sentiments of one concluding paragraph of a letter to an agency manager: 'Let us get all the enjoyment we can out of life and continue to give the best we have to the company.'

A late-marrying bachelor, he was also a lifelong athlete whose collection of golf, curling, and cricketing trophies was the despair and envy of his friends. Described by his gymnastic instructor at the Montreal Amateur Athletic Association as 'neat of body, clear of mind, active and dexterous in movement', he was not the man to be daunted by the challenges of hard times. 'Life assurance,' he was quoted as saying in 1932, 'was organized for stormy weather as well as fair.'

In the late years of T. B. Macaulay's presidency Wood had taken a steadily increasing part in the work of shortening sail. He had had to make great economies, he had had to reduce staff and he had had to maintain morale in the face of decreasing business. He had had, in some areas, actually to decrease business by eliminating unprofitable plans which could no longer support the investment features of the twenties. Yet he had maintained the confidence of the company and the confidence of the public in the company, and he had made headway. By June 28, 1934, he was able to tell an agency conference at Banff that Sun Life, in the four years of the depression, had not only held its own among the three hundred companies then competing on the continent but had advanced to tenth position in the total of business in force.

It was only one of many heartening signs that were beginning to appear. The plague of lapsed policies and the demand for policy loans had begun to abate. Group insurance was rising, a sign of decreased unemployment. The general trend of business was still downward and that would continue for a while, but there was a new sense in the country that the worst was over. There was a new appreciation of the fact pointed out by the Dominion government's Superintendent of Insurance that, even in the deepest year of the depression, 'no holder of a life, fire or casualty insurance policy in Canada lost any portion of the protection provided by his policy through the inability of any company to honour its obligations'. The *Financial Times* of Montreal, in a headline on January 19, 1934, had been even more succinct. 'Life insurance,' it said, had been 'a steady rock in a troubled sea'.

9

'One Steady Grind'

BETTER DAYS

'For the last six years,' wrote Arthur B. Wood to John A. Tory on December 29, 1936, 'it has been just one steady grind, with no let-up whatsoever.' To his old friend, who was now Supervisor for Western Ontario, he was permitting himself the luxury of a mild complaint. He had, however, some good news to go with it. As the end of this year approached, officials of the company were looking forward to the figures of the annual statement 'with much more pleasurable anticipation than at any time since 1929'. There was no longer need for a government valuation of the company's securities; they could meet the test of the market. 'We have claimed from the outset,' Wood wrote, 'that our book values in the aggregate were fundamentally sound, that all we asked was to be left alone, and that as soon as recovery got well on its way the market values would soon rise again to equal or exceed the book values, and that is the situation today . . . the outlook for the new year is really very bright.'

It was not so bright as it seemed, for there were still troughs ahead; and it was only bright at all by comparison with the recent past. The inherent soundness of the company's financial position was at last justified, but its business was sharply pruned and its growth near to a standstill. Economy and consolidation had become the rule everywhere. The final stage of the great Head Office building had been completed in 1933, and the central tower now rose to its full height of twenty-six storeys, graceful, functional, and dominant on the skyline of Montreal. Many of its floors were occupied by tenants, but others were still left vacant and unfinished. Sun Life's Head Office staff, now at two thousand, was down by almost a third from the total of 1930, and the field force had also suffered reduction.

For four years there had been no dividends to shareholders, and considerably reduced dividends to the holders of participating policies. Total insurance in force, which had fallen to $2.7 billion by 1935, would not again cross the three-billion mark for another seven years. The decline in new insurance, which seemed to have been arrested in 1936, was to resume in 1938 and by 1940 bring the total to the lowest figure in sixteen years. Business in the United States improved and faltered again with a sickening regularity. Depression in Canada was to return fitfully and linger stubbornly, with improving conditions in the east balanced by drought in the west. The years of the steady grind were far from ended, and the long road of recovery was leading only to war. Yet in spite of it all Wood knew whereof he spoke. By the time he came to present the annual statement for 1936 a watershed had been passed.

The fact was indicated most dramatically by the increase in the company's surplus. After four years of hovering at a figure below $6 million, it had risen to $18 million with a supporting contingency reserve of $10 million. Equally significant was the change in distribution of the company's holdings. 'Since 1931,' Wood pointed out, 'we have invested exclusively in fixed-interest-bearing securities, with a view to bringing our investment account into more balanced proportions.' The result was that only 33 per cent of the assets were now in common stocks, while 42 per cent were in bonds. At the same time, in the face of a general decline in interest rates, the company had increased its own rate of return on mean invested assets to a figure of 4.29 per cent, an improvement for which the increased dividends on its common stock holdings were largely responsible. Most tangible sign of all of improving conditions was that it was now possible, after a lapse of four years, to increase the scale of dividends to the holders of participating policies and make a moderate allotment to shareholders.

REDISTRIBUTION OF PROFITS

Another significant announcement made at the annual meeting had been preceded by much discussion and a long period of study. The division of profits between policyholders and shareholders had been a matter of concern to the directors for some time. The 95 per cent allotted to the holders of participating policies since 1897 was five percentage points higher than the figure required by law, and for thirty years it had seemed to be generous enough. Policyholders were receiving dividends on a steadily increasing scale and by 1929 Sun Life could fairly claim that its net cost of insurance, as represented by premiums less dividends, was the lowest of any company on the American continent. Yet at the same time, with the large earnings of the period, even the 5 per cent of profits that went to shareholders represented a handsome return on their capital. It had invited criticism in Canada and it had attracted American speculators to the shares of Sun Life. At one period, with the stock soaring to fantastic prices and a significant percentage of it held in American hands, there had seemed to be an actual danger of control passing to the United States.

With the onset of the depression that danger had passed, though only for a little while. Instead, there were new difficulties. As the company rebuilt its strength and reduced its dividend scales it had sacrificed one of the factors that had made for growth in the past. The Sun's representatives in the field could no longer claim that their company offered insurance at the lowest net cost. The competitive position had slipped badly and it was time to think of restoring it.

Wood, in discussing the question with the directors, approached it as Robertson Macaulay had done fifty years before. He pointed to public criticism of the high returns to shareholders. He pointed to the competitive position of the men in the field. But he staked his case above all on the basic nature of the business. 'A life assurance company . . . occupies a position in relation to its policyholders which has the character of trusteeship. The company is the medium or the instrument through which the policyholders are brought together for their mutual benefit . . . life assurance is, in fact, a co-operative enterprise in which the policyholders are entitled under their policies to participate in the benefits derived from successful management.' In all this the capital supplied by shareholders was of gradually decreasing importance and the return should also decrease.

The paid-up capital of Sun Life was now $2 million. It had been built up since the company's inception, about half by payments in cash and half by allotments from the shareholders' proportion of profits. Including these allotments, the total of dividends to shareholders in the sixty-five years of the company's life had been $7,585,686. Over that period, and for a company of the world-wide stature of Sun Life, it hardly presented a picture of swollen returns. It was actually less than one twenty-seventh of the dividends paid to policyholders over the same period, and to the shareholders of a railway or an industrial corporation of comparable size it might well have seemed small. But Sun Life was not a railway or an industrial corporation, and its shareholders were not the sole owners. They were the trustees and managers for thousands of participating policyholders, and as the company continued to grow the shareholders' equity continued to decrease. Their share of the profits, though still supported by law, tended to become excessive. It had been the one basis for criticism in the late years of the twenties, and now in the lean thirties Wood proposed to remove it. 'My considered opinion,' he concluded in his memorandum to the directors, 'is that a substantial reduction should be made at once in the shareholders' percentage of the surplus derived from the participating branch.' That opinion was adopted by the board and it was announced at the annual meeting that profits on the participating branch of the business would henceforth be divided in the proportion of 97½ per cent to policyholders and 2½ per cent to shareholders. 'We wish to show by our actions,' said Wood, 'that when we say that policyholders' interests are paramount, this statement has a real meaning.'

RECOVERY IN THE FIELD

All this was heartening news for the company's managers in Canada and the United States. They had been invited to attend the annual meeting on February 9, 1937, and for the next three days they were in consultation with officials at Head Office. They had brought with them, as expected, an imposing list of problems. Sales had decreased and staff had decreased with the coming of hard times. Among the buying public, even as times improved, the need for insurance competed at a disadvantage with the need to replace all that had been worn out and gone without during the depression. Though new policy loans were decreasing sharply, there was a dragging residue of old, unpaid loans that was resulting in lapsed policies. The reduced dividend scales were a serious difficulty and in addition to that, because of declining interest rates, Sun Life had increased the premiums on new business under some of its plans. The field men who found it hard to sell all forms of insurance found it even harder now to sell non-participating life, or plans in which the investment feature predominated.

Yet, if the field force was reduced and its difficulties increased, there was evidence enough from the managers that morale was still high. Retrenchment was not quite over but growth was beginning again, and the confidence was there to support it. These men who had lived out the depression with the Sun believed in the Sun; they were prepared to accept the changed conditions of the times. They welcomed the current increase in the dividend scale, but were not promised and did not expect that it would very soon be repeated. Once again, and with renewed stress, insurance must be offered to the public for its basic purpose: as a contract providing protection, a duty owed to his own by a prudent man. It would mean harder work and longer waiting for results, it would mean a change in the agent's attitude and a change in the mood of his prospects, but the time was ripe for both. 'Conditions are now favourable,' Wood had said at the annual meeting, 'for the gradual increase of our agency forces by the addition of carefully selected agents.' Care would certainly be necessary and a high degree of training, and beyond that guts and fibre; but the managers left for their offices with no doubts that they could find the men.

TOWARDS THE NEW WAR

When the managers left, they were buoyant and confident again but there was to be no spectacular progress, either for them, or the company, or the country. Through 1937, and on to the outbreak of war in 1939, the legacy of the depression continued. In the field, agencies were slowly rebuilt yet new business faltered in the face of stagnant conditions in the country generally. At the heart of operations there were new and perplexing difficulties. Out of the huge necessities of relief came higher and higher taxes. The hardships of many borrowers brought cries for the remission of debt, often approaching talk of repudiation. Both were symptoms of the times and both had to be accepted, though there remained the question of degree. On both counts the business of insurance suffered and the companies encountered criticism when they tried to state the facts. They were not mighty monoliths sitting on vaults of gold. They were aggregations of policyholders, each with his private stake in the company's fortunes. The policyholder was the real taxpayer, the policyholder was the real lender of the funds the company advanced. It was he who carried the weight of increased taxes as an increase in the cost of his insurance. It was he who would share the loss in remission on a borrower's loan, and he would frequently be no better off than the man he relieved. It seemed difficult to place the nature of insurance squarely in the public mind. Yet, in some fields, there was constructive and hopeful effort.

The Dominion Housing Act, passed in 1935, was a first move to cope with the great shortages in Canada, and insurance companies were looked to as a principal source of funds. Sun Life responded immediately and by the end of the year was making its first loans. By the end of 1938 the total on the company's books stood at $8,644,000, representing approximately 30 per cent of all loans made under the act. In 1939 David Ball Mansur, Sun Life's Inspector of Mortgages, who had taken a deep interest in the workings of the plan from the beginning, resigned to become General Superintendent of the newly-formed Central Mortgage Bank. As forerunner of the Central Mortgage and Housing Corporation, of which Mansur was to be the first head, it had barely got under way by the time the war came. But the work, though interrupted, was of great importance for the future and had already accomplished much. It had demonstrated both the importance of insurance funds and the willingness of the companies to co-operate in meeting the needs of the country.

Between 1931 and 1939 no new offices of Sun Life were opened in the United States, and thirteen were closed. Abroad, there was a general constriction and decline in the company's business which had begun before the depression and was to continue afterward, largely because of changes in local conditions. Sun Life either withdrew or terminated the writing of new insurance in Colombia, Spanish Honduras, El Salvador, Chile, Nicaragua, Mexico, Peru, French Guiana, Surinam, and in several areas of the Levant and the Middle East. Most important of all was the termination of business in Japan in 1938. Balancing the withdrawals, there had been expansion in South Africa, where new offices were opened in Durban and Johannesburg in 1931. In Great Britain also, by 1938, there was a moderate increase in business. By that time, however, over all growth and all the hopeful symptoms that were pointing the way to recovery, the threat of war was darkening.

The company entered upon the last year of peace with conditions still difficult but with no doubt that its own strength was restored. Among the directors there had been few changes. E. A. Macnutt had been elected to the board in February of 1934, Robert Adair had died in 1937 and Morris W. Wilson had succeeded him. In 1938 J. W. McConnell had resigned from the directorate of Sun Life, and from fourteen other directorates, upon assuming the presidency of The Montreal Star. John A. Tory, retiring as Supervisor for Western Ontario, had been elected a director to replace McConnell. Among the senior officers of the company, H. P. Thornhill was now Joint Treasurer, Edward E. Duckworth had become Comptroller, and F. J. Cunningham had succeeded H. Warren K. Hale as Secretary.

For all these senior men, as for all the staff of the company, there had been hard and testing years. Yet the ordeal had been worth while. 'It made us,' George W. Bourke was to say years later. He himself, as Wood's right-hand man, had carried much of the burden and acquired seasoning in the process for the problems that lay ahead. E. A. Macnutt, the tall, shaggy-browed expert on investment and finance, had risen to his full stature in coping with the difficulties of the period, and he had found in Thornhill and in J. W. Brown, the Assistant Treasurer, the strong support he needed. Brown, in addition to his abilities in the investment field was one of the ranking tennis players in the Dominion, while Thornhill, a tall, affable Englishman who had come to Sun Life in 1923 after a considerable experience in finance, was at home in any company and graced any company. To American associates he was known familiarly as 'The Dook', while in Arthur Wood's opinion 'he would have made a very fine-looking bishop'. Allied with their efforts was the knowledgeability of C. S. V. Branch;

and Frederick James Cunningham was a Secretary who would be long remembered. A graduate of McGill and a medallist in civil engineering, he had turned to the challenge of actuarial science and had not been cramped by the difficulties of the new profession. Wide-minded and easy-going, as much at home with men as he was with figures, he fitted naturally into a group of senior executives who could play together as well as work together. It was perhaps the secret of their toughness through the gruelling days of the depression, though it was not always without friction. When he was retiring in 1946, E. A. Macnutt recalled the golf tournaments of those days in which all went well for the low-scorers like himself 'until we appointed an actuary to the handicap committee – after that no good player ever had a chance'. But he also recalled that at a time when many executives of many companies were breaking down, 'no one in our company had to take a rest'.

Whatever the reason, Sun Life had weathered the depression, but the new test was at hand. In August 1939, while the air was thick with rumours, Wood embarked on a tour of the company's offices in Western Canada. He had reached Edmonton when the imminence of war became clear, but he decided to carry on as far as Vancouver. From there, on August 31, after a tense luncheon and a brief reception, he turned back for the east. When the telegram was handed to him on Sunday, September 3, he was still on board the train. There was a state of war between Great Britain and the German Reich, and the last days of the peace were running out in Canada.

10

The Second World War

ON THE BUSINESS FRONT

Of all periods in the company's life, it was perhaps through the years 1939 to 1945 that it became most closely integrated with Canada and at the same time most deeply involved in the ramifications of a world-wide business. It was a part of the mobilization of North America, it shared in the ordeal of the British Isles, and much of its work went down in the wreckage of the Far East. It sacrificed earnings and it spent brains; its young men and many of its young women set their lives at risk. Upon Sun Life, as upon all businesses and most men, total war descended, demanding a blank cheque. Nothing could be withheld for everything was needed, yet at the same time there could be no abdication of function or of primary responsibilities. The business of life insurance, so vital in many fields of the nation's economy, still had to go on.

That it did go on was one of the many achievements on a home front where miracles became the order of the day. Year by year, along with the mobilization and arming of men, with the building of ships and planes, with the vast expansion of agriculture and the vaster expansion of industry, insurance policies continued to be written, insurance premiums continued to be paid, and insurance funds to be invested. For millions of policyholders the stability of protection remained. The benefits of maturing insurance poured out their great waves of purchasing power. And the investment funds of insurance companies, directed into the war loans, became a principal source of support for the allied effort. So far as Sun Life was concerned, in spite of depleted staffs and riddled agencies, it emerged at the end of the war stronger than at the beginning. And it could fairly claim that in the exercise of its proper function it had done essential service. It had accumulated thousands of new policyholders protected by millions in new assets, and it had forged in the process one of the weapons of war. Sun Life had helped with the launching and headed the subscription list of every one of the Canadian Victory Loans, and its total holdings of bonds of the allied nations amounted by the end of the war to $650 million, more than half of its entire assets.

At home and abroad, the carrying on of the business went hand in hand with the work of fighting the war. Directors and senior staff were called away, became absorbed in new duties, leaving a double burden on those who remained. Towards those who entered the services there were new responsibilities, gladly assumed by the company. Early in September 1939 Arthur B. Wood announced that married men and single men with dependents would receive an allowance equal to the difference between their company salary and their service pay and allowances, while two-thirds of the difference would be made up to single men without dependents. To all who entered the services full salary would be continued for a month after enlistment, and throughout the duration of service seniority would be maintained while retirement allowances, death benefits and contributions to staff insurance policies would all be continued by the company. The Sun Life man would find his position waiting when he returned from the war and in the meanwhile, to the fullest extent possible, the financial sacrifice would be eased.

During the same period, while the young blood of the company was flowing into the services, the years were taking their toll of older men. It was a time of many changes in the company's board. Sir Herbert Holt and Senator Lorne Webster died within a day of each other in September 1941; the Honourable Raoul Dandurand died in March 1942; and in April of that year the death of T. B. Macaulay closed a long chapter in the company's history. Sir

Edward Beatty, who had served in wartime as representative in Canada of the British Ministry of War Transport, died an exhausted man in March 1943; and the most tragic loss of all was the death of Arthur B. Purvis. As chairman of the British Supply Council in North America, Purvis had directed the great flow of war material that crossed the Atlantic to Britain and had been largely responsible, in the opinion of C. D. Howe, for the developments that led to Lend-Lease. With that work accomplished and much else still to do, he was returning from England in a plane of the R.A.F. Ferry Command on August 14, 1941, when he was killed in a crash on take-off.

In replacement of these men the company added distinguished names to its board. The Honourable Charles A. Dunning, who had been a brilliant success as federal Minister of Finance, became a director of Sun Life in 1941. Harold Crabtree, industrialist, G. W. Spinney, Bank of Montreal, Arthur Cross of Dominion Steel and Coal Corporation, and the Honourable F. Philippe Brais were elected in 1942, and W. M. Neal of C.P.R. in 1944. The new members of the board, in common with the sitting members, found much of their time and energy taken up by the work of war. They were all prominent in the life of the country and they were all required, with hundreds of others like them, for the giant mobilization which was transforming industry, rushing supplies to the war fronts, financing the great effort, and sustaining public morale. On the board of the Allied War Supplies Corporation there were three Sun Life directors, Charles A. Dunning, Harold Crabtree, and Ross McMaster. Morris Wilson, president of the Royal Bank, had been since 1940 the chief representative in North America of the British Ministry of Aircraft Production, and he later succeeded Purvis at the head of the British Supply Council. The success of the national War Loans testified to the brilliant talents of G. W. Spinney as a banker and financier, and he was supported in Quebec by the energy of E. A. Macnutt, the prestige and influence of Taschereau, and the eloquence of Brais. Brais, one of Quebec's distinguished lawyers and a notable figure in its public life, also served as vice-chairman of the Wartime Information Board. Dunning was in demand everywhere and seemed to meet every demand, in spite of delicate health. Morris Wilson, with his work done at last, returned to civilian life a worn-out man and died, a casualty of the war, in 1946.

Arthur B. Wood, fourth President, 1934-50.

British Administrative Office of Sun Life of Canada after a German high-explosive bomb made a near miss – October 1940.

·SUN·LIFE·ASSURANCE·COMPANY·OF·CANADA·
LA COMPAGNIE D'ASSURANCE-VIE·SUN·LIFE·OF·CANADA·
SIÈGE SOCIAL-MONTRÉAL

SERVICE DE LA CAISSE
S. H. ALLAN, CAISSIER
E. S. COPE, CAISSIER ADJOINT
TÉLÉPHONE: PLATEAU 3131

IMMEUBLE SUN LIFE
SQUARE DOMINION
MONTRÉAL

VEUILLEZ TOUJOURS INDIQUER LE NUMÉRO DE LA POLICE AU SUJET DE LAQUELLE VOUS ÉCRIVEZ

REPRESENTANTES:—GRAN BRETAÑA
EL CONDE DE ALBEMARLE.
EL BARON CHARLES DALRYMPLE.

INCORPORADA 1865

R. MACAULAY, Presidente.
S. H. EWING, V.-Presidente.
T. B. MACAULAY, F. I. A., Actuario.
F. G. COPE, Sup. de Agencias

"SUN LIFE" Compañía de Seguros sobre la vida, del Canadá

(SUN LIFE ASSURANCE COMPANY OF CANADA)
OFICINA PRINCIPAL, MONTREAL, CANADA.

AL HACER REFERENCIA DE UNA PÓLIZA, CÍTESE EL NÚMERO.

DEPARTAMENTO DEL PERÚ, ECUADOR Y BOLIVIA
OFICINA EN LIMA: BAQUIJANO, 309.—CASILLA, 69.—TELEFONO, 576.

Gerente: PEDRO DÁVALOS Y LISSÓN.
Cajero: DAVID HENRIQUEZ DE LEÓN.

No.________

SUN LIFE
ASSURANCE COMPANY
OF CANADA
HEAD OFFICE: MONTREAL

Sun Life
ASSURANCE COMPANY OF CANADA
HEAD OFFICE · Montreal

WORLD WIDE
SERVICE
SECURITY

·SUN·LIFE·ASSURANCE·COMPANY·OF·CANADA·
·HEAD·OFFICE ESTABLISHED 1865 MONTREAL·

A sampling of the hundreds of Sun Life letterheads in use over the past 100 years.

A pair of peregrine falcons attracted world attention by nesting on a top level of the Sun Life Building in Montreal for seventeen years, from 1936 until 1952, 'undoubtedly the first authentic instance of peregrines nesting on a man-made structure in a city'.

ommander J. L. Harries, RCN(R), hose wartime exploits as a Navy frog-an earned for him the George Medal nd Bar, O.B.E., and Legion of Merit U.S.), was the Company's General lanager for Great Britain and Ireland hen he retired in 1966.

Major G. D. A. Biéler, D.S.O., M.B.E., of Head Office, a hero of World War II. Captured after fifteen months with the French Resistance, he died in 1944 before a Nazi firing squad.

Lieut.-Col. T. C. Lewis of Head Office, prominent on Sun Life's own Honour Roll, rose on active service from private to the command of a brigade before he was killed while leading his men in October 1944.

Members of the Sun Life 'Eager Beavers' Troop Show who entertained the armed forces in Britain and the Continent during a four-month, 12,800-mile tour of the war areas of Europe in 1945.

ROLL OF HONOUR

Of the younger members of Sun Life, 1,076 enlisted for active service. Forty-four gave their lives, many others were wounded, and some spent years in prison camps. There were, moreover, among the many who received awards for special services, three at least of the notable heroes of the war. The names of 'Tommy' Lewis, 'Guy' Biéler, and James Leslie Harries stand out with a special lustre on the Honour Roll of the company.

Lieutenant-Colonel Thomas C. Lewis, D.S.O., was a clerk at Head Office who had joined the army as a private shortly before the war. A natural soldier whose qualities of leadership came out almost at once, he moved up quickly through the ranks and was soon on active service. By October 1944, as the Canadians advanced to the crossing of the Leopold Canal in Belgium, he was not only a lieutenant-colonel but was acting in command of a brigade. In this capacity, during the fierce fighting at the canal, he was killed at the head of his troops. 'Colonel Lewis,' said Major-General C. B. Price, 'was absolutely outstanding as a commander and, had he lived, would undoubtedly have proved one of Canada's foremost military leaders.'

Major Gustave Daniel Alfred Biéler, D.S.O., M.B.E., an expert linguist, had been Chief Translator at Head Office and had gone overseas with the Régiment de Maisonneuve. In England he had volunteered for special service with British Military Intelligence, and in November 1942 he was parachuted into Northern France to work with the Resistance. His back was injured on landing, but in spite of severe and constant pain he insisted on carrying on. For fifteen months, disguised as a French workman and co-operating with members of the Resistance, he sabotaged canals and waterways, disrupted German transport, and supplied London by wireless with a flow of information. In January 1944 the wireless fell silent; Biéler had been taken by the Gestapo. Of the nine months that followed little is known and few care to speculate, but when his end came in September 1944 it was marked by a grim testament to the strength and courage of the man. 'This is the only instance known to us,' wrote the British officer who was charged with the duty of informing Biéler's widow, 'of an officer being executed in such circumstances by a firing squad with a Guard of Honour.'

In the war at sea a memorable record was compiled by Commander J. L. Harries, who survived his many adventures to become General Manager of Sun Life for Great Britain and Ireland, and who retired only in 1966. Commissioned in the Royal Canadian Navy in 1940, Harries went on loan to the Royal Navy and commanded a minesweeper in the Channel during the worst period of the air raids on British ports. He soon transferred to the even more dangerous business of clearing blocked harbours and de-fusing parachute mines. As one of the first frogmen, his work in these deadly and intricate operations earned him the George Medal and Bar 'for great bravery and undaunted devotion to duty in the face of danger'. For the same or similar work performed in the harbours of Europe during the invasion he was awarded both the Order of Officer of the British Empire and the American Legion of Merit.

THE WAR IN ENGLAND

There were many other such men who went out from the offices of Sun Life to face the dangers of war around the world. In England, however, war came home to the staff, was shared by everyone, and was a part of the daily work. In London, during the last week of August and the first three days of September 1939, the great administrative building on Cockspur Street was evacuated, except for a few of the personnel in two departments, and turned over to the military. It stood throughout the war with its lower section protected by high brick blast walls and its windows shattered by bomb fragments from the occasional near-miss. Yet the company's business went on, with hardly an interruption, some ten miles away.

Early in 1939 arrangements had been made to take over the buildings and grounds of Carn Brea School in Bromley, Kent. It was here, with files, office equipment, desks, and staff crowded into the classrooms of the school, with many housed in Nissen huts on the grounds, and with the large central residence for dining and recreation, that Sun of Canada lived out the war in Britain.

Most of its men and many of its women were away in the services; those who remained, with as many additions to the staff as could be recruited locally, spent much of their time at air raid drills and in piling sandbags and digging shelters. Night after night the drone of bombers came, the alarm was given by spotters on the rooftops, and the rest of the staff trooped down for hours in the shelters. Yet somehow, day by day, they went on with their work. They were still at it, and still casual about it, as the flying bombs appeared towards the end of the war. 'Ever since these confounded doodle-bugs started arriving in the middle of June,' came a letter from Carn Brea on September 6, 1944, 'it has been a case of going home from the office, having a bite of food and getting out again in uniform . . . we have been out five and six nights a week helping to clear up the mess.'

THE FAR EAST

Since the company did not do business on the continent of Europe it suffered no losses there. In the Far East, however, the scene of its pioneering in early days, the results of the war were painful. There were few investments to be threatened and the amount of insurance in force represented only 2.7 per cent of the company's total volume. Yet it was substantial and it was valued, and it would never be quite recovered. At the outset of the war Sun Life had business in the Philippines, Netherlands East Indies, Malaya and Singapore, Burma, China, Hong Kong, and Thailand which amounted to some $80 million. It came to a total standstill as the territories were overrun by the Japanese. Offices were closed, company managers and secretaries were interned or lost their lives, and the local staffs were scattered. It was upon the native employees of the company that the tragedies of occupation fell heaviest of all, yet there were many examples among them of loyalty and devoted courage. Maung Pwa, who is now a pensioner of the company at the age of seventy-six, was at that time a senior employee in Sun Life's Rangoon, Burma, office. Just prior to the arrival of the Japanese he personally arranged the transfer of the company's records by oxcart some four hundred miles north to Mandalay. Here, through much of the war, he saw to their preservation in an underground dump behind Sun Life's Mandalay premises and, in spite of aerial bombardment, fire, and the attentions of looters, was successful in having many of the records recovered and moved to Bombay.

The company itself, as the curtain of the occupation closed down, was completely shut off from contact with its people in the Far East. But it was not without resources which it determined to use to the full. In the case of policyholders who had fallen into enemy hands, the first step was to get in touch with those, other than the insured, interested in these policies. Frequently this was a Canadian, British, or United States employer who was agreeable to continuing the premium payments. Meanwhile, the wives and families of policyholders, evacuated prior to the war, were scattered all over the world; and the company embarked on a search which, with the assistance of Canadian Trade Commissioners in Australia and New Zealand, located thousands of such people in India, Australia, South Africa, England, and North America. In many cases the Sun Life policy was their only source of funds, and these were made quickly available. Later, hundreds of others who had been evacuated or had escaped from the war zone came unsought to Sun Life offices, usually in desperate need and with nothing to support their claims. They were dealt with on the simple basis of trust. Policy service was resumed in accordance with their signed statements, and policy loans were advanced to wives and dependents with no security but the assumption of good faith. It was an assumption that was fully justified at the end of the war. The company's records in the occupied territories, preserved very often at great pains and risk, did not reveal a case of fraud or misrepresentation.

THE UNITED KINGDOM SECURITY DEPOSIT

At home and around the world there were few branches and few levels of the war effort in which Sun Life or its people were not somehow involved. The Sun Life Revue, a civilian concert party, organized, staffed and trained at Head Office, entertained the troops at many camps in Canada. Towards the end of the war, changing its name to the 'Eager Beavers' to avoid any commercial implications, it was launched on a triumphal tour of the British Isles and Europe. The Sun Life Employees' War Aid Association sent thousands of parcels of clothing, comforts, and medical supplies to soldiers overseas. The Sun Life building in Montreal housed the headquarters of Canada's Military District No. 4, and from January

1941 to May 1944 the government-in-exile of Luxembourg was established in three rooms on the eighth floor. Meanwhile, beneath all the normal and abnormal activity of the great building, there was other work going on. It was known only to a handful who were sworn to complete secrecy and who were engaged in spite of themselves in one of the melodramas of the war.

On July 18, 1940, with France under the heel of the Nazis and the British Isles threatened by invasion, the Chancellor of the Exchequer had informed the House of Commons that 'American and other securities which are marketable outside Britain . . . are being held in Canada pending their realization'. The flat statement meant a good deal more than it said. Some $5 billion in stocks and bonds, most of them the private property of British subjects, had been taken over by the government and shipped across the Atlantic. They were to be sold in North America to meet the cost of the war and along with them, in a series of fast voyages by heavily escorted warships, had gone the bulk of the British gold reserve. The gold ingots were now reposing in the vaults of the Bank of Canada, while more than two thousand boxes of securities lay three storeys underground in the sub-basement of the Sun Life building in Montreal.

The first of the shipments, unloaded at Halifax from the cruiser *Emerald,* had arrived at Bonaventure Station in Montreal on the evening of July 2 in a heavily guarded special train. Shortly after midnight it had been trucked through sealed-off streets to the east entrance of the Sun Life building. From there, with the trucks surrounded and the basement ramp lined by a cordon of watchful, armed police, the crated boxes of securities had been carried down to what was known as the Buttress Room. It was not to be their permanent home, for that was still building. The building was going on, night and day, as other shipments came in to join the first. By July 28, however, the place was ready.

It had been requested by the Bank of England during the hectic days of June. What was required, President Wood had been informed, was some three thousand square feet of absolutely secure vault space with working space adjoining it for at least a hundred people. The space Sun Life could provide by clearing out its workshop and storeroom area deep down in the solid rock of the island. But the other requirements were formidable. Plumbing and ventilation and electrical equipment would all have to be installed some fifty or more feet below street level. An 'absolutely secure' vault meant heavy concrete walls and tons of supporting steel, and there was no steel to be had. Concrete could not be poured in the low basement area. There would have to be a vault door with all its delicate mechanisms, and there were no such doors available. A job that would require months, even with proper materials, would have to be done in weeks.

Faced with this series of impossibilities, and always in complete secrecy, a half-dozen men of the company had gone to work. They had got steel by ripping up some two miles of the trackage of an old, disused railway. They had borrowed a vault door from The Royal Bank of Canada, which had met the request by robbing one of its branches. They had set up two powerful compressors on the street outside the building, and had blown 800,000 pounds of sand, cement, very fine stone, and water down a long airhose into the forms for the walls. By July 28 they were finished. The vault door was in place and in operation, set into steel-ribbed concrete walls three feet thick, and behind the walls were nine hundred four-drawer filing cabinets, all crammed with securities. They were protected by an alarm system so delicate that it would record the sliding of a drawer, and they were guarded night and day by twenty-four men of the Royal Canadian Mounted Police who ate and slept in the building.

The next stage of the work had already begun. The securities were in Canada to be marketed as necessary in meeting the costs of the war, and it seemed likely for a while that their total value in dollars would have to be realized. At the same time the British owners of the securities must be reimbursed in sterling. This meant, first of all, the cataloguing and itemizing of vast masses of certificates which had been bundled in haste and without much order into the crates for sea transit. A. S. Craig of the Bank of England had come to Canada with four colleagues, accompanying the first shipment. With the help of the Bank of Canada, the Foreign Exchange Control Board, and Sun Life he had recruited a Canadian staff of some 120 retired bankers, investment executives, clerks, and secretaries. These were now at work on what was known officially as the United Kingdom Security Deposit and was in fact one of the largest, strangest, and most secret stock and bond businesses in the world.

All through the summer of 1940 and on into the spring of 1941 the staff of the operation lived their own queer private life. They were bound by an oath of secrecy. They came down from the main floor by a single private elevator, showing their passes as they entered and again as they left. They emerged into a large, well-lighted office outside the vault, with armed guards everywhere. Squads of secretaries sat at tables, busily clipping bonds, tabulating securities, putting them into bundles. Seventy miles of tape, it was reported afterward, went into the work of tying up the individually-owned parcels of securities. Six thousand 'query slips' had gone out from the sub-basement to London in the straightening-out of details. Meanwhile, under the direction of senior officials, the work of marketing went on.

The trading operations of the United Kingdom Security Deposit came to a virtual close with the advent of Lend-Lease in March 1941. But the securities themselves remained in the Sun Life sub-basement for four more years, one of the best-kept secrets of the war. It was not until August 1945 that the bonds and stocks went home and the story reached the newspapers.

By that time, on every level of the Sun Life building and through all the branches of its business, recovery was under way. Staff was returning, men were thinking ahead. Tired senior executives were beginning to relax and reflect. Arthur B. Wood, a President in his mid-seventies, had cheerfully borne a daily increasing work-load. George W. Bourke, the veteran of the earlier war, had remained at his right hand, though perhaps a little envious of Alistair M. Campbell. Campbell, drafted to Ottawa at the beginning of the war to assist in the work of the Foreign Exchange Control Board, had soon gone on from there into active service. He was now an artillery officer as Bourke had been, and after a lively war he was getting restless in Europe. Bourke was getting restless at home; he wanted Campbell back. There were many others of the Sun who were now restless in the service, and they were all wanted back. There was going to be much to do.

11

'An Institution of the Average Man'

THE PRESIDENT'S REVIEW

For Sun Life, as for most people and most businesses in North America, the late months of 1945 brought a confusion of happy homecomings and a thousand problems of adjustment. With 1946 came the general settling down and sorting out. Problems began to resolve themselves as men took up the tools of their trades once more. The shape of the post-war era began to emerge. It was possible to look about and look ahead. To that task Arthur Wood addressed himself as he came to the end of the year, and the result was a notable speech delivered to the annual meeting. It was a broad and heartening review, not only of the state of the company but of life insurance in general.

Already, a year before, he had dealt with the great progress made in the liberalization of the insurance policy and the extension of insurance coverage. The world-wide unconditional policy pioneered by the Sun in 1880 had long since come into general use in the industry. So had the various systems of loans, cash value allowances, and automatic extensions in case of premium default which assured to the policyholder 'the full equity in his policy at all times and under all conditions'. The range of plans was constantly widening to meet the varying needs of individuals, and at the same time there were many policy options available. The life insurance agent was no longer merely a solicitor of new business; he was a trained financial adviser who studied the needs of his prospect and selected the plan to meet them. Sub-standard health was no longer a bar to insurance, and the under-average life could now generally acquire a measure of protection on fair and scientific terms. With all this, and with the growth of group insurance, pension plans, and annuities, the place of the life insurance industry in the economy of North America was vastly enlarged. In Canada, where life insurance in force per head had been $20 in 1875, it was $850 in 1945, while the equivalent per-capita figure in the United States was $1,100. More than half of the entire population of Canada and the United States had acquired a direct interest in life insurance, either as policyholders or as beneficiaries.

Speaking a year later, with the figures for 1946 before him, Wood could point to impressive advances in this trend. For life companies in Canada, the United States, and Great Britain, the first full year of the post-war era had brought a substantial increase in the volume of new insurance. In the case of Sun Life, the advance over 1945 was 44 per cent. It was due in part to a high and well-distributed level of national income, to a shortage of consumer goods, and to the increase of the field forces of the companies as men returned from the services. But there were other factors more permanent and more significant. 'The war period,' said Wood, 'has also thrown into bold relief the vital importance of life assurance, while the great contribution made by the companies to the successful prosecution of the war has brought them a measure of public confidence never before equalled.'

There was another important area in which the interests of insurance companies were combining more and more with the national interest. Public health was a matter of concern to everyone, and it affected the cost of insurance. Improving mortality rates meant ultimately lower premiums and more protection for more people. They were the object of constant study by all insurance companies, and there was no doubt that mortality rates were declining. Sun Life's mortality rate for 1946 had been the lowest on record. It had improved by 30 per cent from the years just prior to the First World War. Through medical research, health education, and health legislation, all of which had been assisted and supported by insurance companies, the young and the middle-aged had been given longer life. The death rate from childhood diseases had been reduced. Tuberculosis, typhoid, pneumonia, and influenza, the great killers of fifty years before, were beginning to be tamed. Heart disease and cancer, the diseases of later life, remained as the principal enemies; and it was in the battle against these that the insurance companies were now joining. In 1945, Wood told his hearers, 139 American and ten Canadian companies had established a Life Insurance Medical Research Fund which was to provide contributions of $600,000 annually over an initial period of six years. Already, with the assistance of the fund, research experts were at work in American and Canadian laboratories. Life insurance, with its constantly expanding place in the national economy, was also a greater instrument in the promotion of public health.

Turning more particularly to Sun Life, Wood noted first the scope of its operations, 'with agencies forming a cordon extending around the world'. Canada now accounted for 32.7 per cent of the business in force, the United States for 41.5 per cent, and the British Department, which included the United Kingdom and Eire, for 12.1 per cent. These were the three largest of the five departments into which the company was organized for purposes of administration and supervision. Of the other two, the Eastern Department, which comprised Egypt, South Africa, India, the Philippines, Hong Kong, Singapore, and other countries in the Far East, represented 9 per cent of the business; while the remaining 4.7 per cent was in the Western Department, which embraced the West Indies, Cuba, Puerto Rico, Argentina, and certain other countries in Central and South America.

Both in the Eastern and the Western Departments there had been a shrinkage since the peak years of the twenties. Much business had been lost in some areas and more might yet be lost, not only from the effects of the war but because of the changes in political and economic conditions. Yet much remained, some would return in time, and even in territories which might be permanently vacated Sun Life had no cause to regret its work as a pioneer. The investment had been recovered and invaluable experience acquired; there were few areas of the world and few international problems with which the company was not familiar. More than that, a priceless memory had been left of fair dealing and faithful adherence to contracts. 'The world-wide activities of the Sun Life of Canada,' said Wood, 'have been and still are an important factor in making the name of Canada well and favourably known and in paving the way for trade connections, for the Company was firmly established in many countries long before the advent of the trade commissioner.'

In the territories of the Far East which had been occupied by the Japanese, Sun Life representatives had returned as soon after the war as the authorities would permit their presence. The office in Shanghai had been reopened in late 1945; there were Sun Life men in Manila by October, and a few months after that in Hong Kong, Singapore, Netherlands East Indies, and Siam. Everywhere, the first work had been to ascertain claims that had arisen during the occupation, find the beneficiaries, and make immediate payment. Many policies on which premiums had been long unpaid were still valid because of the automatic nonforfeiture provision, and in the reinstatement of these the company's regulations had been stretched to the limit. Interest rates had been reduced on policy loans and premium arrears, while in the case of lapsed policies every means had been adopted to see that the policyholder got the last shred of his equity. With all this, for many months there had been little attention paid to the writing of new business; yet new business was coming. It would not return in China, where the Shanghai office had had to be closed again at the end of 1946. But in Singapore and Malaya and in Hong Kong and the Philippines volume was building again on the base of a renewed and accumulating fund of good will.

In all fields of its operations the company was now showing the results of the long period of consolidation which had begun with the coming of the depression and continued throughout the war. The total of insurance in force at the end of 1946 was $3.5 billion, which represented an increase of only some $465 million over the total for 1931. Yet in the same period the company's assets had more than doubled, advancing from $624 million to $1.3 billion. The distribution of assets was also changed strikingly, with bonds now making up 77.7 per cent of the portfolio and common stocks only 6.3 per cent. The investment in mortgages, too, though it represented only 4.7 per cent of total assets, stood at the highest figure in the company's history and had been of major importance in the field of housing. In Canada, since 1935, Sun Life had made over 13,000 loans under the National Housing Act for a total of

$52 million. There would undoubtedly be many more, and on housing loans as on all mortgage loans interest rates were low. Low interest rates were one of the pressing problems in every field. But the company was immensely stronger now, with assets better distributed, and was prepared to meet all problems. The large borrowings of governments had ceased with the end of the war, and there would soon be a healthy shift to older channels of investment. 'Once again,' concluded Wood, 'life assurance funds will flow to meet the needs of industry and commerce by providing long-term loans, making mortgages to home-owners, and purchasing the obligations of public authorities.'

EXECUTIVE CHANGES

The seventy-six-year-old President was now approaching the end of his long career. In the actual direction of the company George W. Bourke had played a major part since 1944, when he became General Manager as well as Actuary. In June 1946, with the retirement of E. A. Macnutt, there had been a general changing of the guard and several of the senior executives were settling into new roles. Bourke now joined the board as Managing Director and would soon take on the added duties of Vice-President. H. P. Thornhill was Treasurer. Alistair M. Campbell, six months home from Europe, had become Actuary. J. A. McAllister, an ebullient westerner who had come to Head Office from Edmonton in 1927 and had been appointed Director of Agencies in 1944, remained in that post, while J. B. Mabon, who had been Associate Actuary since 1932, became Underwriting Executive. Amid all the problems of post-war transition the team was taking shape that would pilot the company onward through the next stage of its growth.

THE UNITED KINGDOM

Two members of that team, George W. Bourke and J. A. McAllister, embarked with Wood for England in June 1947. The purpose of the mission was wholly misunderstood, as George Bourke recalls, by one of his shipboard friends. 'Going to England to wind up the business?' the man inquired, with the thought of the much-bombed, austerity-straitened islands in mind. 'No,' said Bourke crisply, 'we're going to England to expand it.'

The confident tone was justified, not only by the experience of the war just past, but by the whole long history of Sun of Canada in the United Kingdom. The company which had had to fight for its very name when it opened its first small London office in 1893 had gone on to carve out a foothold for itself in the face of long-established and very powerful competition. By the time of the First World War its business was large and firmly based throughout the British Isles, but that war had so riddled its agency forces that in early 1919 it had not a single agent in the whole of the London area. Recovery had come again, but recovery had been followed by the depressed years of the thirties, and the company had suffered here as in North America. Yet each difficult period had been the prelude to new advances. There had been the toughness and durability to surmount all obstacles. There had been determined management and resourceful field forces eager to rebuild and expand, and the same was true again at the end of the Second World War. For eighteen years much of the power and drive behind the company's operations had been provided by H. O. Leach, who had been General Manager for Great Britain since 1929. Widely experienced in Canada and the United States as well as in the United Kingdom, he had borne the burdens of the war with his accustomed sang-froid. They had told on his health and he was now approaching retirement, but he was leaving a good legacy to the men who would carry on. The proof of it lay in that war-battered but still handsome building on Trafalgar Square, once more housing a busy company staff. It lay equally in the figures of the annual statement, where British business in force at the end of 1946 amounted to over £97 million, representing more than 12 per cent of the company's world-wide total.

Expansion was in the air as the first post-war agency conference of Sun Life's British Division gathered in Brighton on June 15. The 342 men and women present made up the largest company group ever assembled in the British Isles. Among the men from the Administrative Office some had the sleeve band of a Carn Brea fire-watcher among their cherished souvenirs. Among the three hundred field representatives many had been young clerks when they left to go into the services, and they were in the field now because of the plan of assistance and training offered them by the company on demobilization. The hardships of the past linked them, and achievement in spite of hardship buoyed them up. Somehow, throughout the war, Sun Life's British Department had maintained a constantly increasing volume, and the sales for 1946 amounted to some £12 million, the highest figure on record. It was an eager, confident, forward-looking group of men to whom the company's executives spoke, and their words were as confident as their listeners.

George Bourke, in particular, seemed stimulated by the air about him. 'Had I not been an actuary,' he said, 'I think I would have been a salesman,' and he went on to sell these salesmen on the scope of their opportunity and the immense resources behind them. 'Counting our field force and the employees in Head Office, London Administrative Office and our 115 branches, the Sun Life has today an active personnel of about 6,300 men and women.' It had more than one and a quarter million policyholders. It was the largest Ordinary life company in the British Empire and the ninth largest on the American continent. 'We are, of course, the largest Canadian company . . . our business in force is 25 per cent greater than the total for the next three Canadian companies combined.'

THE QUARTER CENTURY CLUB

The executives came home from England with no doubts about the future of the British Department. Here, as in North America, agency forces were rebuilding, new training programs were taking effect, and newly-acquired staff was melding smoothly with the old. The company was going forward. But it was also looking back to what it had built on, the inner resources of loyalty that had sustained it through many trials. On April 24, 1947, at a dinner in the Head Office auditorium, 178 employees of the company had gathered to inaugurate the Sun Life Quarter Century Club. Each of them had spent twenty-five years or more of his life with the company, and the average was thirty-one years, carrying back the general memory over all that had been accomplished since the First World War. Altogether, throughout the world, there were 457 employees who were entitled to induction into the Quarter Century Club, and during the course of the year they were welcomed at other occasions and received the clock or silver tray that had been made the symbols of membership. They were greeted with good words that acquire an enriched significance as the ranks of the club grow:

Men who fare the road together through a quarter of a century achieve a companionship of their own. When their journey has been for a great social institution, bringing good to fellow human beings, the companionship is richer. In that truth is the genesis of the Quarter Century Club of the Sun Life Assurance Company of Canada.

The Sun Life is not the handiwork of a few, but the creation of many. Men and women, down the years, have served its aims with integrity and sympathy, and with conscious pride in its worth. They have been inspired by a comradeship of common milestones and memories. As the years pass, too, others join their ranks, but the great traditions remain unchanged – traditions of probity, of good faith, of the honoured word.

THE FIFTH PRESIDENT: GEORGE W. BOURKE

It had long been Arthur Wood's custom to recognize the twenty-fifth anniversary of each employee's service by writing him a personal letter. He had wanted to do more than that; the idea of the Quarter Century Club had been in his mind for a long time, but it had had to be thrust aside by the problems and stringencies of the depression and the many demands of war. That it came to fruition now was a proof that his work had succeeded, and it was work almost done. Through 1948 and 1949 he presided with growing detachment over the group of younger executives who were dealing with newer problems. On February 14, 1950, he delivered his last address to an annual meeting; and on the same day George W. Bourke became the company's fifth President.

There had already been other changes, and more were pending. R. A. Taylor had become Comptroller of the company on the retirement of E. E. Duckworth, and in the same year G. E. Brown had become Personnel Executive. With Bourke's elevation to the presidency, Alistair M. Campbell, F. J. Cunningham, and J. A. McAllister had all become Vice-Presidents. H. P. Thornhill, as Vice-President and Treasurer, was within a year of retirement, and in 1950 he was succeeded as Treasurer by E. R. Alexander. Among the members of the board, John W. Ross had died in 1946 and G. W. Spinney in 1948. W. M. Neal had resigned in 1948 because of ill health, and with 1950 came the deaths of W. M. Birks and John A. Tory. Bell Telephone's Frederick Johnson; Ross Clarkson of Royal Trust; R. E. Stavert, Consolidated Mining & Smelting; A. E. Grauer, B.C. Electric; and J. S. D. Tory, Q.C., the son of John A. Tory – these were the new directors elected to replace the old.

As the new President completed his first year in office, transition had been achieved. With depression and war behind it and the post-war adjustments made, the company at the mid-point of the twentieth century was confronted with other problems of a world in change. There was war in Korea, there was disruption and the threat of more in the Far East and the Middle East, there was fear of inflation at home. Yet every healthy tendency that Wood had noted in his earlier address was being steadily reinforced. Life insurance per capita, both in Canada and the United States, had increased by nearly 30 per cent over the figures he had quoted. The variety of plans had increased, and so had the scope of protection. Nearly one-half of all policies on adults were now being issued without medical examination, yet mortality rates continued their general decline. They were declining in part because of the assistance to medical research, and that assistance was increasing. Life companies in Canada were now supporting studies of polio and of the processes of aging, and were providing research fellowships at university medical schools. At the same time, the investment funds of the companies, released from wartime demands, were pouring out to build houses, advance industry, and support the growth of the nation.

By 1951 Sun Life, as a sharer in all this work, had seen the one and a quarter million policyholders referred to by George Bourke in 1947 increase to one and a half million. For the second year in succession it had increased dividends to policyholders, beginning a long series of increases that would continue for two decades. It was writing new insurance at the rate of $1.7 million for every working day, and for every working day it was paying out to its policyholders and beneficiaries about half a million dollars. Of perhaps even more significance for the long future was the average amount per policy issued in 1950. It had increased to $4,460, compared to the $2,680 of ten years before. It meant that the average man was buying more insurance, and 'the Sun Life of Canada', in the words of Arthur B. Wood, 'is an institution of the average man'.

George W. Bourke, fifth President, 1950-62.

The Coronation procession of Queen Elizabeth II passes the Sun Life Building in London – June 1953.

Selected Head Office personnel receiving six weeks' concentrated tuition in electronic programming, prior to the arrival of Sun Life's first electronic computer in 1957.

12

The Challenge of the Fifties

THE WIDENING RANGE OF SERVICE

'Every year,' said George W. Bourke in 1956, 'important discoveries of mineral resources are being made, new industries are being created, new roads and railroads are being built, electrical power projects undertaken, and now the St. Lawrence Seaway is under construction.' It was a businessman's cool summary of basic conditions, and he might have said much more. Canada, advancing with the forward thrust developed through the late forties, was in the midst of one of the greatest periods of economic development the country had ever known.

Similar conditions prevailed in the United States and the United Kingdom. For Sun Life, as for all life insurance companies, the problems were the problems of prosperity: the matter of keeping pace, widening the scope of service, adjusting older practices to the requirements of a new era. The demand for financial security had never been greater. The challenge to life insurance was to provide new forms of protection, with extended capabilities and with maximum adaptation to the needs of the individual.

Even before 1950 Sun Life had made many significant additions to its wide range of plans and policies. The writing of group insurance increased steadily with the growth and expansion of industry, and a natural accompaniment to this was the group pension plans. More and more, corporations turned to Sun Life for combinations of group insurance and group pensions that enabled them to offer their employees protection while at work and security on retirement. By 1956, with a growing demand for supplementary cover, and with the development of new and more varied plans, there was a further extension of range. On January 1 of that year Sun Life entered the sickness and accident field.

The sale of individual annuities grew as prosperity brought surplus funds to more people. In 1957 federal legislation providing income tax relief on premiums paid against retirement savings contracts was a spur to this type of plan. With the growth of corporations and the increasing complexity of business there was more call for insurance on the lives of executives, for the protection of partnership agreements, and for other hazards dependent on human life. Above all, for the average earner with new means at his disposal there was a host of varying and special needs. The mortgage on the new home, the higher education of children, the maintenance of stable income became paramount considerations that required both special protection and special settlement arrangements. It was the young man with family responsibilities, successful, ambitious, and wanting the most for his money, who forced the pace of the period.

To all this Sun Life responded with variety and flexibility. As early as 1953 more than 30 per cent of its new ordinary business was being sold on plans that had not been available six years before. The trend continued as the company opened new branches, increased its sales force, and intensified agents' training. The representative of Sun Life, said George Bourke in 1956, had become a man experienced in the planning of family insurance needs, in estate analysis, in the principles underlying business insurance and partnership agreements, and in programming for retirement. First and foremost, however, in this 'institution of the average man', he was equipped to assess the specific needs of a client. 'For the great majority ours must be an individual service.' It was also a worthwhile service. By the end of 1957 Sun Life, with $7.7 billion of life insurance in force, had more than doubled the volume of ten years before.

INVESTMENT POLICY

Concurrently with the growth in underwritings came developments in investment policy. Government legislation throughout the period tended to relax some of the restrictions that had cramped the employment of life insurance funds. The so-called 'basket clause' was a notable innovation, through which a life company was permitted to invest up to 3 per cent of its assets in fields outside the prescribed range of securities. This new freedom in the employment of a fractional proportion of its assets was both an evidence of trust in the judgment of its investment personnel and a recognition of the great opportunities of the times. For Sun Life it resulted most significantly in a changed attitude towards real estate investment.

Ever since the bleak thirties existing insurance law had confined Sun Life's holdings, for the most part, to properties necessary to house its own business. There had been little enthusiasm either for the possibilities of appreciation in the value of property or for the prospect of earning revenue. Now, however, as government restrictions were lifted views changed. During 1956 the company placed $13 million in revenue-producing real estate, and by the end of 1957 the total held for investment had risen to $39.8 million. Also, in the same year, construction was begun of the striking new Sun Life building on University Avenue in Toronto.

Within the investment department there was a new emphasis on planning. The long-range forecast of changing business conditions, and the possible distribution of incoming funds to meet them, received more attention. The 'profile' of investments, for as long as five years ahead, became of increasing importance in the company's thinking.

Yet, on the whole, there was little need for change of direction from the policies of recent years. In the older, traditional fields of investment the demand for funds was almost too great to be met. In 1951 alone, capital expenditures in Canada amounted to over $4.7 billion, of which less than $600 million came from abroad. Much of the balance came from the great pool of savings administered by Canadian life companies, and it was this same reservoir that largely supported the economic growth and development of later years. Interest rates, continuously on the rise, made it profitable to invest in the many issues that were offered of industrial, public utility, provincial and municipal bonds, and in commercial and home mortgages. The funds of Sun Life were poured out for the construction of highways, waterways, railroads, mining developments, oil developments, and other great projects occupying the country. They continued, as they had since 1935, to support the building of homes. In this field alone, by the end of 1957, Sun Life's advances to borrowers under the National Housing Act had reached a total of $359 million.

The resources contributed by policyholders had been used for the needs of the times, and they had grown notably in the process. The total of assets, standing at $2.1 billion, had been increased by $500 million since 1950. The surplus had grown to $150 million. And, of greatest interest of all to the participating policyholder, dividend scales had been increased for the ninth successive year.

NATIONALIZATION IN INDIA

The period was not without setbacks, of which the most painful for Sun Life was the nationalization of its insurance business in India. On January 19, 1956, a Presidential Ordinance of the Indian government, later confirmed by an act of the Indian parliament, provided for the taking-over of all life companies operating in the country. Of these, among non-Indian companies, Sun Life of Canada stood first. Its business, which had been built up over a period of sixty years, amounted to the equivalent of some $90 million and was more than fully supported by assets located in India. It had operated from first to last with the good will of the government, and good will continued though political necessities prevailed. Sun Life made voluntary provision for the pension rights of its native Indian employees. Its departing officers, all reluctant to leave, gave every possible assistance to the Indian officials who replaced them.

The terms of the transfer, as finally negotiated, were characterized by the company as 'severe but not entirely unfair'. Sun Life was allowed to retain control and servicing of policies belonging to non-Indians in currencies other than rupees. Some compensation was paid for loss of business, and excess assets were released. Beyond that, however, the door to India was closed, and it was not the end of the process. By September 1957, as it became apparent that Ceylon was inclined to follow the example of India, new business was terminated there.

THE NEW REGIONALIZATION

Many of the agencies that had once formed 'a cordon extending around the world' were now no longer in existence. The business of Sun Life, by the end of 1957, had become concentrated almost entirely in the principal divisions – Canada, accounting for 51 per cent, the United States 34 per cent, the United Kingdom, South Africa, and other Commonwealth countries 13 per cent, with the rest of the world only 2 per cent. Yet, if there was cause for regret in the geographical contraction of the business, there were many compensations. It could be claimed not unreasonably that Sun Life and other Canadian companies had helped to foster the demand and create the conditions that were now making it possible for developing countries of the world to offer their own people the benefits of life insurance. At the same time, in the more advanced regions, they had increased volume enormously, widened their scope of service, and played a part in improving the conditions of life. They were largely responsible for the increased financial security enjoyed by the average man. They could take a measure of credit for the advances in public health, the expansion of medical research, the decline of many diseases. And, with all this, there was still far to go. Life insurance, daily increasing in range and flexibility, was only beginning to realize its potential.

The operations of Sun Life were now centred for the most part in some of the richest, most economically advanced areas of the world. Yet even here, as George Bourke pointed out, the life insurance carried by the average man would provide his family with the equivalent of only one year's income. It was much, but it was not enough; the scope for increase was enormous. It would have to come, as always, in the face of 'this strange inertia toward the purchase of life insurance', but there was no doubt that it would come. 'The reasons for the purchase of life insurance are so compelling that the public should beat a path to the doors of the life insurance companies.' This was not likely to happen, but the pathmakers were there in the persons of some three thousand Sun Life representatives. They were a well-equipped, increasingly successful force, with a justified faith in their product and no fears for the future.

A CHANGING ECONOMY

In Canada and elsewhere, during 1957, the great surge of economic development reached and passed its peak. There was small fear of any serious recession, and no decline whatever in the sale of life insurance. But the demand for capital was beginning to outrun the supply, while the demand for goods and services was bringing the fear of inflation. Businessmen and industrialists were attempting too much too soon, and there were other accompaniments of growth that were not entirely healthy. High interest rates and large profits were accompanied by rising taxes in every field. In the field of life insurance the very success of the industry brought on its attendant criticism, usually uninformed and often damaging. Considerations of undoubted social utility were forcing governments into fields that had long been the private preserves of insurance companies. It was beyond dispute that the conditions of the times justified and demanded a new attitude towards such matters as old age security, pensions, and public health; but they also demanded definition of areas. That problem, with many others, was looming large ahead.

CHANGING PERSONNEL

Among the directors of the company Arthur B. Wood, Chairman of the Board, died in 1952; and in the same year the long career of the Honourable L. A. Taschereau came to an end. J. McG. Stewart, Q.C., elected a director in 1952, died in 1955; and a year later came the death of Harold Crabtree. As new directors, Gordon R. Ball and George Gund were elected in 1952; J. A. Fuller of Shawinigan Water & Power and R. D. Harkness, Northern Electric, in 1954; Albert S. Fraser, Eastern Trust, and Hartland de M. Molson, Molson's Brewery, in 1955. Alistair M. Campbell became Executive Vice-President and a member of the board in 1956; and in 1957 Sir George Bolton, Bank of London & South America, was elected, the first resident of the United Kingdom to become a director of Sun Life.

In December 1957 Edward Ryckman Alexander became Vice-

President, Finance. A graduate of McGill and Harvard, with a brilliant academic record, he had joined the company in 1925 and advanced steadily through a succession of senior posts in the investment department. Already widely known and respected in Canadian and international financial circles, he was to become a director of Sun Life in 1958 and continue for another ten years in charge of the company's investment portfolio. Long associated with Alexander, and now succeeding him as Treasurer, was J. S. B. Pemberton, whose distinguished record in financial affairs included much experience in the management of Sun Life's overseas investments.

At the head of the company's legal department, R. D. Taylor, Q.C., was Vice-President and General Counsel. J. A. McAllister was now Vice-President, Agencies, with W. G. Attridge becoming Director of Agencies. H. F. Gundy was Underwriting Executive, Lachlan Campbell had followed Alistair M. Campbell as Vice-President and Chief Actuary, while Hugh McLeod and J. W. Ritchie had been advanced to the rank of Actuary.

In July 1951, Dr. Cecil Clinton Birchard, Chief Medical Officer, had died after thirty-six years of service with the company. A member of the Royal College of Physicians of London, England, a Fellow of the Royal College of Physicians (Canada), and a Fellow of the American College of Physicians, he had contributed much not only to the advancement of medical practice in the company but to the cause of medicine generally.

Dr. J. Keith Gordon, who joined the company in 1924 and became Medical Director of Sun Life in August 1951, was a man of similarly distinguished ability. A Fellow of the Royal College of Physicians (Canada) he was, like Dr. Birchard, actively connected with the medical work of McGill University and with the Montreal General Hospital. During the Second World War he was in charge of Medical Division No. 1, Canadian General Hospital, Overseas Service. His career with Sun Life, resumed at the end of the war, was to be terminated all too soon by his death in 1959 at the age of sixty-four.

PENDING CHANGES

With the close of the books in 1957 the company concluded its eighty seventh year. Of its success and its vitality there could be no doubt at all. Yet, largely because of these, it was involved in basic changes both to the mechanics of its operation and the very nature of the business. At the annual meeting for 1954 George W. Bourke had informed the policyholders and shareholders that the company was studying the possible use of large-scale electronic computers. Two years later he announced that a computer had been ordered; and by 1957 preparation for the huge task of automating records and procedures was under way. What the President did not announce, and could not publicly discuss, was the approaching mutualization of Sun Life of Canada. The work, for several years past, had occupied much of his days and many of his nights, and it was not yet complete. But that process too was now well under way, and the transformation of the company only a matter of time.

13

Automation and Mutualization

THE FIRST ELECTRONIC COMPUTER

Univac II, scheduled for delivery in 1957, actually arrived at the Sun Life building in Montreal on Friday evening, May 30, 1958. A convoy of four transport trailers which had been almost a week in travelling from St. Paul, Minnesota, pulled up at the unloading ramp to discharge twenty-four tons of disassembled components into the hands of Univac technicians. Installation began at once on the fourth floor of the building, which had been designed as the computer centre and strengthened for the weight of the 'brain'. By August the work was completed and by September the computer was operating.

Some five years of investigation and more than a year of intensive planning preceded the arrival. As early as 1952 the company had recognized the possibilities inherent in new methods of electronic data processing, and had made known its own requirements to the companies developing the equipment. By 1953, as it seemed possible that these requirements could be met, a committee had been set up within Sun Life to study the application of the computer to the various departments of the business. By May 1956, with these studies completed, the order had been given, and actual planning began.

Univac II could perform thousands of calculations per second, with absolute accuracy assured by a system of double-circuitry under which each operation was performed twice and each checked against the other. It could store the result of its work in a 'memory' so compact and capacious that one 1,500-foot reel of magnetic tape could carry the complete data for six thousand individual life insurance policies. Four of the reels, as was found later, could embody the entire record of the 43,000 mortgages in the company's Canadian portfolio. The computer made it possible, in the case of a single policy, to assemble on a three-inch strip of tape all the particulars which were now distributed through many departments of the business, sometimes requiring as many as twenty files. It could transform accounting, simplify statistical work, eliminate thousands of time-consuming procedures. It was obviously a formidable tool, with formidable implications.

These last had been well studied, particularly in relation to staff. Reduction was not a problem and was not considered; one of the first conclusions reached was that, taking into account normal turnover, all those presently with Sun Life would still be required. What had to be thought of was the huge task of changing over the records, the keeping pace with the normal growth of the business, and the training of men and women for new and more challenging work.

'We tried,' says one executive, 'to have an intelligent, human approach to the problem.' The staff were kept fully informed of what was intended. On all departmental planning committees there were both senior men concerned with the broad problems and juniors closely in touch with the detailed work. Innumerable classes, courses, and seminars produced planners, programmers, and operators for the new equipment. The same classes and others stimulated a re-studying of routines and developed new applications of computer methods. There was no pre-judging of the abilities either of age groups or the sexes; and it was found that younger and older men as well as younger and older women accepted training readily and adapted easily and well. It was, moreover, one of the basic principles of the operation that the change-over should proceed on a broad front, maintaining an equal rhythm of advance among all departments.

The results, as they began to appear, justified the approach. There were always 'bugs' to be eliminated, each advance in systems seemed to open the way to another, and the only constant was change. Yet little by little, as increasing streams of data fed in from many departments, the computer centre was becoming the heart of the business. By the end of 1961 it was operating on a round-the-clock basis, and another computer had been ordered. There was a new compactness in records, a new speed and accuracy in the processing of all data, a new freedom to plan because of the elimination of routine. And a staff of whom 'virtually none would go back to the old system' had achieved with the new efficiency a wider interest in their work.

A THREAT TO THE COMPANY

Meanwhile, in the quiet of the executive offices and the board room, a more portentous change was almost completed. It had been ten years in the making, and some of its early foreshadowings went further back than that. T. B. Macaulay, in the late years of the twenties, had warned that the success of the company might attract adventurous speculators. Between January 1927 and October 1929 he had seen the price of the company's stock rise from about $560 per share to a fantastic $4,100, while at the same time the proportion of American holdings increased to about 20 per cent. It had seemed to him a move to take over the company, and he had proposed to fight it by doubling capitalization and distributing the additional stock in Canadian hands. In the four years, however, that were required to obtain approval for such a change, the depression intervened. The Sun Life, by 1931, had legal authorization to increase its capital from $2 million to $4 million, but there was now no point in doing so. The price of the stock had dropped to a low of $145 and speculators who were not bankrupt were looking in other directions. The company, itself battered by the storms of the early thirties, was at least freed of the spectre of foreign control.

That freedom ended with the close of the prosperous forties. On March 16, 1950, when George W. Bourke had been President of Sun Life for slightly over a month, the spectre rose again. Harold Allen, a New York financier, had become a shareholder of Sun Life on March 2, 1950. By March 8 he had written to request an interview, and eight days later he was sitting across from the

President at his desk. Speaking as the owner of seven hundred shares of stock, he advanced a number of proposals which were enlarged at subsequent interviews. They were all based on the premise that, with a change in management policies, Sun Life could make a great deal of money for its shareholders. By October 12 the proposals were reinforced by vague hints of support from other groups who controlled additional stock, and they had come to include not only a large increase in the dividend paid to shareholders but a stock bonus, a stock split, and a seat on the board for Allen. Among numerous other suggestions, Allen was particularly insistent on a change in the company's practice which now allotted 97½ per cent of distributable surplus to the holders of participating policies and only 2½ per cent to shareholders. He was not impressed by the argument that Sun Life had operated on the present basis for thirteen years, that both the company and the government considered it equitable, and that any change in practice might bring a change in the law. Policyholders, he felt, had had all the best of it at Sun Life, and it was time to adjust the balance. Either the present management would do it or a group of dissatisfied shareholders might be forced to take control.

A campaign was well under way that would go on for six years. Behind Allen himself loomed the shadow of a notable brother. 'Wall Street,' said *Time* magazine in its issue of November 20, 1950, 'has seldom seen a nimbler broken-field runner than 47-year-old Charles Allen, Jr. A New York City boy who quit school at fifteen to become a Stock Exchange messenger, Allen learned the Street's ways so well that he parlayed his pocket change into $15 million. With his younger brothers, Herbert and Harold, he built the potent investment banking firm of Allen & Co. They bought up and reorganized the Rockefellers' famed Colorado Fuel & Iron Corporation, Germany's war-forfeited American Bosch Corporation, captured many another plum with their sharp-eyed knack for spotting "special situations".' That knack, it was now clear, was directed towards Sun Life.

THE STRUGGLE TO RETAIN CONTROL

On November 7, 1950, George W. Bourke and the directors of Sun Life reviewed the developing situation. It was considerably less dangerous than it had been a week before, partly because of a telephone call that had been made by Harold Allen. On October 27, with his holdings of Sun Life stock increased to 1,100 shares, he had phoned K. R. MacGregor in Ottawa, the Dominion Superintendent of Insurance. His purpose had been to confirm the fact that Sun Life could legally increase its shareholders' allotment of distributable surplus from 2½ per cent to 10 per cent. That purpose had been accomplished, but the net result of the call was rather different. A statement from the Minister of Finance, the Honourable Douglas C. Abbott, was issued five days later. It took note of the hopes of speculators and issued a clear warning. The practices of Canadian life companies, while they had not been compelled by law, were about to be confirmed by law. Legislation would be introduced 'substantially in harmony with the practices followed by the companies in recent years'; and this, in the case of Sun Life, would establish the shareholders' proportion of distributable surplus at a maximum of 2½ per cent. The effect of the statement was drastic when it reached the markets, and Sun Life shares which had been much in demand at $1,500 had promptly dropped to $1,000.

Nevertheless, if the situation had eased for the moment, the company was still vulnerable. Sun Life's capital of $2 million was divided into twenty thousand shares of a par value of $100. Of these, Allen owned 1,100 shares and claimed that he and his friends controlled 4,000 in all. The claim was perhaps exaggerated, but they were certainly in possession of between 10 and 15 per cent of the company's stock. At the same time, they were pressing for a list of shareholders, with the obvious intention of buying additional holdings. Letters from suspiciously recent purchasers of Sun Life shares were demanding 'better treatment'; and propaganda in some of the financial papers, possibly inspired, was distorting Sun Life's potential as a source of shareholder profits. Allen, in spite of his bruising in the market and his loud protests against the '2½-per-cent law' that was about to be passed, was not abating his efforts to gain control of the company.

He had been refused a list of the shareholders, and would continue to be refused. But this, at best, was a limited means of defence. When inflated prices were offered for the company's shares there were many situations in which sales were likely to be made. Much of the stock of Sun Life had been passed down through generations and was now in the hands of elderly men and women who were faced with estate tax and succession duty problems. Other considerable blocks were held by estates, banks, and trust companies, and by universities and hospitals. With all these holdings, whether because of the need of funds or the proportionately low return on high-priced shares, there would be increasing pressure to sell. And Sun Life itself could do nothing to relieve the pressure because it was not permitted by law to purchase its own stock.

In the face of all this there was the loyalty of older shareholders when the situation was explained to them; and that loyalty was strong. There was the attitude of the government which was fully aware and alert, and sympathetic to the company. Above all, there was the new sense of urgency which the President and the directors shared. It was essential, according to George Bourke, that this problem be settled, not just for the time being, but on a permanent basis.

The search for that permanent basis was the work of the next few years. It was largely in the hands of five men, who came to be known as the 'inner cabinet' of the company. Alistair M. Campbell as Vice-President and Actuary, F. J. Cunningham as Vice-President and Secretary, R. D. Taylor as General Counsel, and J. E. Chandler as Assistant to the President, all shared with George Bourke the weight of responsibility and secrecy that attended every decision. It was upon their loyalty and strength of purpose and steady nerves that the Board of Directors depended, and the confidence was not misplaced.

In March 1951 the capital stock of the company was split into 200,000 shares of a par value of $10. The move, which the company had considered and debated long before Allen suggested it, had only become possible with an amendment to the Canadian and British Insurance Companies Act in 1950. It was believed now to be opportune as a means of spreading the ownership of shares and increasing the difficulties of speculators in acquiring large blocks. Another amendment to the act, also in 1950, permitted the company to amend its by-laws, allowing the board to make changes in the number of directors, within certain limits. This step was taken in February 1952. It brought to the board room two notable men, one as a shareholders' director and the other as a policyholders' director. George Gund, president of the Cleveland Trust

Company, was a large American shareholder, firmly opposed to the plans of the Allen group. Gordon R. Ball, president of the Bank of Montreal, was to be an indispensable agent in the work of preserving the stock in friendly hands. Over and beyond all this, in 1951, came further legislation much desired by the company. An amendment to the Insurance Act in that year permitted the participating policyholders of Canadian life companies to deliver their vote by proxy at annual meetings. In the offices of Sun Life there was prompt action as the law came into effect. Proxy forms, with a letter of explanation, were soon being mailed out and were being signed and returned. They arrived in such volume that by February 12, 1952, the day of the annual meeting, over two hundred thousand policyholders had entrusted their votes to the President.

Neither at this meeting nor at subsequent annual meetings were the proxies actually required. For all the commotion in the stock markets, the shareholder strength of the company remained substantially allied with policyholders in support of current management. Through 1954 and 1955 the price of the new Sun Life shares was pushed up in the markets to as high as $350. Yet neither the Allen group nor a later and larger group to whom he transferred some of his holdings was ever able to acquire more than about 15 per cent of the stock. The turn of the tide came on May 14, 1956, when Allen walked in on George Bourke with an offer to sell his holdings.

They amounted to 14,000 shares, and they were not quite half of the stock in 'enemy' hands. Nationwide Corporation, the other American group which had acquired stock from Allen, was now known to control some 17,600 shares. It was certainly in the market for more, and had made offers to Allen. His asking price of $375 per share was a stumbling block at the moment, but that might disappear. The dilemma for Sun Life was either to secure the stock itself, for which it had no legal authority, or to risk its acquisition by a still more potent 'enemy'.

Beyond this loomed the basic problem of the company, still unsolved. Even if one raid on the stock were beaten back, there was always the possibility of subsequent raids. The solution lay in a transformation of ownership that would remove the stock from the market. Sun Life, by acquiring the right to buy out existing shareholders, would become a 'mutual' company. Capital would be eliminated and ownership of the assets be vested solely in the participating policyholders. In the inner councils of the company, and in discussions with government officials, this had now been agreed on. It was a course for the future, however, which would require changes in legislation generally acceptable to all Canadian life companies, and would take time to work out. It would not avert the present immediate danger.

The situation was made known to the government, and the course adopted by the company tacitly approved. It was predicated on the assumption of a change in existing law, and it was made possible by the efforts of Gordon R. Ball, director of Sun Life and president of the Bank of Montreal. On the understanding that the company would press forward with mutualization, and on the assurance that Sun Life stock held by the bank would be taken over by the company as soon as the law allowed, Ball went to New York and in a long and exhausting session of bargaining with Allen purchased 15,000 shares at a price of $345 per share. The transaction proved to be decisive, for five months later under a similar arrangement between Sun Life and the Bank of Montreal, and at a considerably lower price, the 17,651 shares held by Nationwide Corporation were also acquired. With the threat of foreign control eliminated for the time being, it was now possible to proceed with the final solution.

MUTUALIZATION

By 1957 the last steps were in train. They involved, first, the securing of general agreement among all Canadian life companies that the privilege of mutualization might be desirable. In this work Alistair M. Campbell, who became president of The Canadian Life Insurance Officers Association in May 1957, played a leading part. Agreement came the more easily because of others besides Sun Life who had felt the hot breath from the south. Between 1955 and 1957 the control of five of the smaller companies had passed outside Canada, and even some of the larger were worried by raids on their stock. By September 1957 the general meeting of minds, which had been laid down by the government as essential to legislation, had been secured. On November 25, 1957, a bill to permit the mutualization of Canadian life insurance companies under

Alistair M. Campbell, sixth President, 1962-70, and now Chairman of the Company.

The 'New Look' of downtown Montreal. In centre: Dominion Square and the Sun Life Building.

SOME NOTABLE MACAULAY CLUB PRESIDENTS:

Harold Charlap, Philadelphia, held the presidency on five separate occasions.

Samuel (Chummie) Hirschmann, Johannesburg, another five-time holder of the Macaulay Club presidency.

Macaulay Club presidents Edward Lord, Tokyo (*left*), and John W. Gordon, St. Catharines, Ontario (*right*), both earned the Club's top office on three different occasions.

A group of the Company's executive officers with George W. Bourke (*centre*) on the occasion of his completion of fifty years with Sun Life – May 1969.

Canadian sculptor Louis Archambault's 1½-ton bronze 'Sunburst' dominates the entrance hall of the Company's building on University Avenue, Toronto.

The Sun Life Centenary Carillon, world's largest, was enjoyed by millions who visited Expo 67 in Montreal. In foreground: the Console. Background: Levis Tower, where the electronic equipment and stentors were located.

Anthony R. Hicks, seventh President,
elected February, 1970.

certain explicit conditions was introduced in the House of Commons. There was little discussion of the measure and no serious opposition, and on December 20, 1957, the bill received Royal Assent.

The company had now the authority to purchase its own stock at 'a fair and reasonable price'. On March 6, 1958, in consultation with federal insurance authorities, this price was agreed on. The shareholders of Sun Life would be invited to sell their holdings to the company at a price of $325 per share.

The price and the necessary by-law to authorize purchase of the shares were ratified at a special general meeting called by the company on May 6, 1958. The purchase of shares commenced on May 27 after official sanction by the Treasury Board of Canada was received. By the end of the year 82 per cent of the shares had been acquired and by July 15, 1959, with 90 per cent of the stock turned in, the sale of the remaining shares had become mandatory at the end of a six-month period. On January 15, 1960, the company became the owner of its entire capital stock. On that day, also, J. S. D. Tory, the last member of the board serving as a shareholders' director, resigned in that capacity and was re-elected as a policyholders' director.

It remained for the stock acquired to be written down to its par value of $2 million and then retired and cancelled. This was completed on December 20, 1962, and Sun Life of Canada became a mutual insurance company entirely owned by its policyholders.

For almost ten years the defence of the company's integrity and the achievement of mutualization had been the dominant and demanding concern of George W. Bourke. It was a fitting climax to a career that had brought him some of the highest honours in his profession. A Fellow of the Institute of Actuaries (Great Britain) and of the Actuarial Society of America, he had also been vice-president of the society, twice a member of its council, and had served a term as president of The Canadian Life Insurance Officers Association. Now, with his work nearing conclusion, he had reached the age of retirement. He had, in fact, passed it, but had been persuaded by the Board of Directors to remain for several months. On November 6, 1962, however, six weeks before the final, formal act in the transformation of the company, the convenient time came. On that day he was elected Chairman of the Board, and was succeeded in the office of President by Alistair M. Campbell.

14

'An Age of Rising Expectations'

ALISTAIR MATHESON CAMPBELL

The sixth President, as he entered on his term of office, was a man of fifty-seven. Born at Strachur, Argyllshire, educated at Inverness Royal Academy and at the University of Aberdeen, he had graduated at twenty-one as a Master of Arts with first-class honours in mathematics. At twenty-two, while he was continuing in his chosen subject as a highly regarded Research Scholar at the University of Aberdeen, he had made the acquaintance of a personnel officer of Sun Life who was travelling in search of specially promising recruits. The meeting had been arranged by the Senior Professor of Mathematics, who considered that his young protégé fulfilled all requirements, and the result had been an invitation to join the Sun Life in Canada. Campbell had accepted, and commenced as a student actuary in 1928.

Both the opinion of the professor and the hopes of Sun Life had been borne out. Alistair M. Campbell was now a Fellow of the Institute of Actuaries (Great Britain), and a Fellow and Past Governor of the Society of Actuaries in the United States. Like his three immediate predecessors he had served a term as president of The Canadian Life Insurance Officers Association, now known as

The Canadian Life Insurance Association. With technical qualifications of the highest order, he had also a rich and broadly based experience. He had seen the peak of the twenties as a junior clerk, and come to responsibility amid the trials of the early and middle thirties. During the period of consolidation and rebuilding that preceded the Second World War he had established himself as a highly valued officer and a man marked out for advancement. The war had come as a break in his career, not entirely unwelcome. Still in his middle thirties, he had gone first to a complex and demanding assignment with the Foreign Exchange Control Board and then, on completion of that, to more active service in the Canadian armed forces. Late in 1941 he was posted to the 1st Field Regiment, R.C.H.A., in England. As an artillery officer he fought through the campaigns in Italy and Holland, and he finished his military service as a captain on the Canadian staff in Germany.

Returning to Sun Life in 1946, after an absence of six years, he was called on almost immediately to assume the post of Actuary. His responsibilities widened with the growth and development of the company through the post-war period; and from the early fifties onward much of his time and energy, like that of George Bourke, was employed in directing the battle against the threat of foreign control. In all the developments that led to mutualization, and particularly in the later phases, his knowledge, his resourcefulness, and his talent for negotiation played a large and vital part. He had done much to build Sun Life and to make it a mutual company. Now, as the first President wholly responsible to policyholders alone, he would be required to set new courses. Yet there would be no change in essence from the tradition of fine leadership that had characterized the past. As he himself was to say a few years later, speaking of the company, 'Initiative, enterprise, imagination and the will to venture into new ground at some risk have been the keystone of our progress.'

THE NEW DEMANDS

There had already been steady gains through the late fifties and early sixties, and more were on the way. All were keyed to 'an age of rising expectations' which would be noted by the Economic Council of Canada in 1966, and which had begun years earlier and would continue to the present day. People were demanding more of industry, more of technology, more of all the processes that were changing their lives. Automation and education were linked in a rising curve; the additional knowledge required for new machines meant more years in the schools and universities, a later start in business life, the need of commensurate rewards in a shorter time. Increasing productivity and a changing social philosophy promised more leisure to the old. In the country's work force the percentage of young men and young women was steadily increasing. They were better educated, longer trained, more alert to their opportunities, and they were marrying earlier and forming families earlier. They wanted much for their children – more than ever before – and the functions of life insurance increased proportionately. In the same way, as the span of the working life became shortened by early retirement, there was more need of pensions and provision for old age.

To all these varied stimuli the response of Sun Life had been flexible and energetic. In 1959 the company had completely revised its premium rates for new business in Canada and the United States. By 1964, after sixteen successive years of annual increases in dividends to the holders of most classes of individual participating policies, its net cost of insurance was once again one of the most attractive in the industry. Its growing field force, constantly refreshed by wide and intensified training, was kept abreast of conditions and the problems of the average man. The average man himself became a subject of closer study as the company reviewed relations with policyholders and simplified policy forms to make the contract easier to understand. Sun Life extended its work in the field of public service with the issuance in English and French of a series of pamphlets on 'Values In Education', which were soon in demand by millions in the schools and homes of the country. At the same time increasing attention was given both to young policyholders whose insurance requirements would change with marriage or the birth of children, and to those whose earning power could be affected by ill-health or injury. By 1962 the Sun Life range of plans and policies included a 'Family Options Benefit' which enabled the man under forty to add protection as needed without evidence of insurability; and by 1965 the disability benefits of its group plans of health insurance had become available in individual policies.

VARIABLE ACCUMULATION FUNDS AND INVESTMENT POLICY

Group insurance itself was in a period of rapid growth, and a particularly significant advance came with an amendment to the Canadian and British Insurance Companies Act in 1961. The change made possible the funding of pension plans through equities and mortgages as well as fixed-interest securities, and Sun Life promptly introduced its Variable Accumulation Fund Group Annuity contract. Through this plan a corporation with a large group of employees could allot its pension contributions, in a proportion set by itself, among an equity fund, a fixed-income fund, and a mortgage fund, all administered by Sun Life. By the end of 1967, after only six years of operation, variable accumulation fund assets had risen to $88 million.

With a widening range of underwritings came developments in investment policy. Here also the company responded flexibly to new conditions. In 1961, with the establishment of a mortgage office in London, it prepared to expand its holdings in the United Kingdom. Its interest in prosperous South Africa was also growing. From 1963 onward there was a significant increase in the portfolio of Canadian, American, and British common stocks, and the investment in real estate for revenue continued to rise. Legislation was widening the field of insurance investment, secondary industry was becoming of increasing importance, and in the older, traditional fields of bonds and mortgages new practices were evolving while demand was never-ending. Everywhere, the work of employing the funds of the company became more complex, more sophisticated, and more selective. New techniques of analysis came to be used, some of them based on new electronic equipment. Profiles of basic policy, projected years ahead, guided the work of special investment committees. The committees themselves, each one responsible for a single area of investment, constantly reviewed conditions, adjusted holdings, and maintained the cardinal principle of security with diversification. 'Savings,' said Alistair Campbell in 1964, 'do not automatically flow into productive investments. . . . The channelling of life company funds into remunerative investments for the policyholders and at the same time into areas of economic development requires imagination, experience and judgment.' It was the old challenge that had always faced the company, and in a time of new complexities it was being met with new resources.

By the end of 1967, after five years of operation as a mutual company, it seemed apparent that all challenges were being met. Sales of new life insurance, which had first risen to over a billion dollars in 1959, amounted in 1967 to $1.8 billion. Total insurance in force was $15.5 billion, and was made up of more than 3.9 million individual life policies and group life certificates. The company's income in 1967 was well over half a billion dollars, and the amount paid out in benefits was $279.3 million. At the same time the net cost of life insurance was being steadily reduced. With assets of $3.2 billion earning an average return in interest of 5.89 per cent, Sun Life was now preparing, for the nineteenth successive year, an increased scale of dividends to the holders of most classes of participating policies.

GOVERNMENTS AND THE INSURANCE FIELD

On all these aspects of growth another factor had been intruding from the late fifties onward. This was the entry of governments, on a large and increasing scale, into the fields of health insurance, hospitalization insurance, and pensions. In 1958 some Canadian provinces enacted measures to provide group accident and sickness insurance. By 1961 the proliferation of hospital insurance plans had begun. In 1962, with the introduction in Saskatchewan of a compulsory government health insurance scheme, and with much discussion of the same in other areas of North America, the general trend was established that would lead to medicare. The discussion of pensions paralleled that of insurance, and in January 1966 the Canada and Quebec pension plans came into effect.

There could be no quarrel with the ideal behind the developments. So far as existing resources made it possible, the citizen of Canada was to be protected against the financial catastrophes of illness and the misery and degradation of poverty in old age. It was the ideal of the insurance companies, expressed in so many words on many occasions. 'The insurance industry in Canada believes that an adequate health care plan must be made available to all Canadians, regardless of their age, the state of their health, their occupation or where they live,' said Campbell in 1963. Speaking on pension plans a year later, he made it clear that disagreement with governments was not on first principles. 'The industry is conscious of the great importance of adequate basic pensions, but is anxious that pensions not be assigned more than their proper relative importance in overall plans for individual welfare.' The debate on social security, long, continuous, and still not wholly resolved, turned largely on means and methods.

It could be argued, and very frequently was, that the insurance companies were motivated by self-interest; they would lose a good deal of business. Yet that loss, even in the field of pensions, was peripheral and almost irrelevant. The field of life insurance was still so wide, the unfilled needs so great, that losses in one sector could soon be made up by increased effort in another. The real and basic objection to government plans lay in the danger the companies saw of an unbalancing of the economy. When health and hospitalization and medical care were 'free' to all, all would pay by their taxes. The contributions of millions who had adequate resources of their own would be lost not only to the companies but also to the general treasury. For those who could not pay there should certainly be free care – and the life companies had submitted plans to governments that would make such care possible. They had not surmounted the difficulty of determining means to pay, but they still held to the principle of insurance scaled in cost to the individual's resources. In the matter of pensions they had some doubts as to the country's ability to support the rate established, but again the real objection went deeper still. If the proportion of national savings that went to pensions became unduly large, then the proportion for life insurance might become unduly small. In terms of the individual, a man who was adequately protected to the end of his own life might leave his widow and children ill-provided. It was with such doubts as the plans came into effect, and not with any prospect of serious losses, that Sun Life adjusted itself to another age of change.

CANADA'S CENTENNIAL YEAR AND THE PROSPECT AT ITS CLOSE

The company had approached the year of Canada's centennial in its usual mood of optimism. It wore a new symbol, adopted in 1965, in which the old device of the sun had a tree centred at its heart, symbolizing growth and reward. There had been ninety-seven years of growth and reward now, and there was much cause to join in the national celebration. Sun Life shared with other life insurance companies in producing 'Man and His Health', one of the most popular theme pavilions of the Universal and International Exhibition of 1967, Montreal, Canada – generally known as Expo 67. On its own account it provided the Sun Life Centenary Carillon, the world's largest, to Expo 67; and the 671 bells of the great electronic instrument rang out daily from historic Levis Tower on St. Helen's Island. Removed at the close of Expo to a home in the Sun Life building, they are still heard by thousands as a relief from the noise and bustle of downtown Montreal.

During the ten years between 1957 and 1967 there had been numerous changes in the Board of Directors. Carl Riordon, Ross H. McMaster, the Honourable Charles A. Dunning, J. S. D. Tory, A. E. Grauer, and Gordon R. Ball had all been lost by death. Arthur Cross, Frederick Johnson, Ross Clarkson, George Gund, and Albert S. Fraser had retired from the board, having reached the company's retirement age for directors. As new directors, V. W. T. Scully, Steel Company of Canada, and E. R. Alexander had been elected to the board in 1958; G. Arnold Hart, Bank of Montreal, in 1959; H. Roy Crabtree, manufacturer, in 1960; Colin W. Webster, industrialist, in 1961; the Honourable James Sinclair of Lafarge Cement in 1962; Louis Hébert, Banque Canadienne Nationale, in 1963; and Frank M. Covert, Q.C., J. Herbert Smith of Canadian General Electric, Marcel Vincent of Bell Canada, Herbert H. Lank of Du Pont of Canada, and Gilbert W. Humphrey of Hanna Mining Company (becoming the second U.S. director) in 1966. M. M. Walter, Royal Bank of Canada, and R. A. Emerson of C.P.R., who had joined the board in 1960 and 1966 respectively, had each regrettably died within months of their election.

As the hundredth year of Canada came to a close, Sun Life of Canada was approaching its own centennial. In a world where rapid change was the order of the day there was much need for vigilance and sufficient cause for anxiety. Throughout North America the urbanization and industrialization, the new technologies and the new government measures that were changing the face of society were also creating an enormous demand for capital. The same was true in Europe, and there was limitless demand in addition among the underdeveloped nations. The world was shrinking with the advance of communications, the aspirations of men were everywhere growing, and the productive resources necessary were not keeping pace. It made for inflation and strained money markets and widespread political unrest, and these would be chronic conditions for years to come. The remedies lay far off, in the restraint of governments, the reform of monetary systems and the accumulation of new pools of savings. In the meantime, however, there remained the administration of available resources, as wisely, as scientifically, and as beneficially as possible. It was a major function of governments and of all large investors; it had always been the function of life insurance, which protected millions of policyholders by the wise use of the funds. It was doubly important now, and doubly challenging. 'In this respect,' said the President of Sun Life, concluding his address to the company's annual meeting on February 13, 1968, 'a vigorous, expanding life insurance industry can continue to serve a vital national purpose.'

15

At the Hundredth Year

THE APPROACH OF THE SEVENTIES

In his address to the annual meeting on February 11, 1969, Alistair M. Campbell looked back over a successful 1968 in which many of the company's records had been surpassed. But he also looked forward along the road that led to the seventies. 'The capital shortage,' he said, 'is not a transitory phenomenon in the economic scene.' It was an acute and basic problem which had hardly yet been grasped in its full dimensions, and which still tended to be aggravated by every factor of growth.

In the Canadian work force there was constant and rapid expansion of the age group between twenty and thirty-five; and the oncoming wave of youth required thousands of new jobs, which required capital to create them. Young people who were marrying and forming families must borrow for housing and transportation and many domestic needs. Capital was required in immense and increasing amounts to supply the schools, roads, electricity, telephones, and other essential services of growing modern communities.

Each advance of technology involved large capital investment, and this too was a constantly accelerating process. It would not halt, and it would still continue to be accompanied by rising expectations. Particularly in the great cities, whose growth was due in part at least to technology, there were huge and increasing demands for renewal and redevelopment.

Beyond this, and looming over conditions in the affluent western world, were the new ambitions and necessities of the underdeveloped nations. The young countries competed at a disadvantage with the demand for capital in the home markets of the more developed nations, and the surplus left for export was very small. It could not be allowed to remain so. 'We cannot overlook the demands for capital for underdeveloped nations. . . . If this worldwide problem is not solved, it can only lead to world unrest and tragedy.'

Against these necessities were the growing perils of inflation, intensifying the capital shortage. In many countries of the world a task of the highest priority was to halt inflation and restore confidence in the future value of currencies. Yet this in itself would produce no new resources. The great pools of capital so necessary for future growth must come, as they always had, from the accumulation of new savings.

For the life insurance industry in Canada this work was becoming more difficult because of the tax policies of governments. High income taxes and high estate taxes, while they tended towards social equality, tended also to reduce savings, since it was those in the upper brackets who were in a position to save the most. In the same way, the Canadian government's policy of taxing life insurance companies on the life business conducted in the country, while based on grounds that were understood, tended to reduce the savings in the private sector. The difficulties would have to be accepted, and be met by the development of new methods. Over many years, and in the face of many fundamental changes in public policy, life insurance companies had continued to provide protection at a decreasing cost while at the same time increasing the supply of capital available for investment. They would have to go on with that, and they would have to go on as before, through change and adaptation to new conditions. 'In this way,' said Sun Life's President, 'they will continue to enlarge their service.'

EQUITY-LINKED POLICIES

One notable enlargement was already under way at the time he spoke. Since 1961 the success of Sun Life's Variable Accumulation Fund Group Annuity contract had encouraged the company to study the possibility of individual policies based on the same principle. These studies were now completed and some of the plans prepared. Early in 1969 the first equity-linked policies were offered in South Africa, based not on guaranteed protection but on units in a Sun Life investment fund. On September 1 a trio of 'Sun Fund' policies was announced in Canada, and on October 1 the 'Maple Leaf Growth Plan' was introduced in the United Kingdom through a wholly-owned subsidiary company.

The products varied by region but the principle remained the same: to give a new range and potential to the policyholder's dollar. Thousands already having insurance protection desired also to participate through equity investment in future economic growth. They could approach this new goal by way of the variable accumulation fund policies; and the fact that they were administered by Sun Life with its immense resources and its many decades of investment experience added much to the prospects of success.

Variable accumulation fund plans have been, in the words of one executive of Sun Life, 'a watershed in the insurance industry'. They have attracted a new segment of the general savings, and they have proved successful to date in putting those savings to work. In its literature introducing the plans, however, the company has been careful to point out that equity-linked investment carries an element of risk. Markets have a downside as well as an upside, and the strongest portfolio of securities can be affected by general conditions. 'We strongly recommend,' it advises potential investors, 'that . . . you do not overlook the importance of guaranteed dollar insurance and annuity contracts in planning your overall future financial security.'

LARGE SALES AND 'MASS MARKETING'

Conventional protection retains its supreme importance and the major part of the company's effort goes still, as it always has, to the enlargement of that sphere. In this work, too, there have been many changes of emphasis in recent years. On the one hand, because of the growing complexity of business and tax problems, there has been a considerable increase in the demand for very large policies. Each of these presents its own special problems and requires and receives the attention of Sun Life officers who are experts in the fields concerned. On the other hand there is the 'mass marketing' of protection in average amounts; and more and more of this is now being provided through the means of group insurance. In addition to companies and corporations, many professional associations and labour unions are now organized to take advantage of group protection, while at the same time the range and extent of benefits available under group policies are being constantly widened. Here too, for the representative of Sun Life, a vast amount of expertise is required in many varied fields.

DEVELOPMENTS IN INSURANCE COUNSELLING

A common problem in connection with group insurance lies in the fact that employees of a company are not always aware of the substantial fringe benefits which in fact they are receiving. To help solve this, Sun Life in 1968 inaugurated its Employee Benefit Service. By arrangement with the insured company, a team of Sun Life experts is established on the premises for the period of time required to have a personal interview with each employee. In the course of this interview the employee is given a clear picture of all staff privileges and benefits, including group coverage, to which he is entitled. Very often such knowledge is found to be an eye-opener, improving company morale. At the same time, in many cases, the individual is stimulated by a better knowledge of insurance to re-examine his provisions for financial security and broaden his own range of personal protection.

INDIVIDUAL BUSINESS

This additional service to men and women insured under group policies parallels the extension of the process of individualizing the company's ordinary business. More and more, as the training of its representatives becomes deepened, broadened, and diversified,

Sun Life is aiming to provide the exact 'mix' of protection suited to particular needs. It must take into account the measure of basic security which is now provided through government pensions and health insurance and often through group insurance. It must go beyond that to assess the total requirements of an individual life. With a range of plans and policies which can be adapted to almost every imaginable situation, the work of the Sun Life man is now primarily a matter of analysis and understanding. Flexibly, imaginatively, and sympathetically, the plan of insurance must be designed to take into account the present resources and the future plans, hopes, and ambitions of the prospect.

THE AGE OF THE ELECTRONIC COMPUTER

All this, which might have seemed an impossibly complicated process a few years ago, is now moving with the help of the electronic computer into the realm of practical, everyday routine. The insurance industry is one of the largest users of computers in North America, and Sun Life has long been a leader in the field. It has now moved through successive phases to a third generation of equipment that dwarfs all previous capacity. The administrative work of the company has been transformed. Its underwriting and medical divisions make daily use of the computer in assessing risks. On the investment side of the business the data that affects decisions is stored in computer 'banks', and computerized information makes possible an instant analysis-in-depth of almost any problem. In the direction of personnel and in methods of training, computerized information gathered from the behavioural sciences is constantly put to use, and just as constantly is being updated to keep pace with new developments.

Many applications now received by the company are rated by computer methods. Nearly all policies are actually computer-written. All policy information is stored in the computer bank. An electronic Family Planning Service applies the growing capabilities of equipment to the growing complexities in the field. The Sun Life salesman, immersed in his client's problems, has normally prepared a form of 'estate analysis'. He can now forward this data to Head Office where it is processed through the computer, and the result that goes back to him is a fully worked out plan. He is enabled to offer his client, on the basis of the information submitted, the most advanced assessment of the protection suited to his needs. This service, constantly expanding, will be a striking aspect of growth in the years ahead. Most of the company's offices in North America are now connected with Head Office by telecommunication, and the day is in sight when they will deal with the computer directly.

Yet, with all this, nothing will change in the basic objectives which led to the introduction of the first computer in 1958: to promote efficiency, to save time, and so to increase concentration on the human problems of the business. In the matter of underwriting, for instance, where much of the simpler rating is now done by the computer, the medical thinking that sets the basis for the rating must always be better informed, alert to current conditions, and conversant with every development in the field of health. The doctors in Sun Life's medical division have been and are leaders in their profession, devoting at least as much time to hospitals and to actual practice as they do to company business. For all their work, both within and without the company, the availability of computerized information relating to the world of medicine is an important professional aid.

In the same way the company representative, Sun Life's man in the field, has his capabilities heightened by the new means and methods. He is a product of special training which is continually refreshed and advanced by the latest in modern equipment and modern techniques. He is kept alert and aware of changing conditions. He has access to the company's great store of computerized information and to its almost limitless resources in the way of analysis and statistical calculation and specialized planning. But he is not de-personalized by any of this; he is only better equipped for the new demands of his profession. His basic resources are still consideration and understanding and a liking for people. His product is still security and his greatest achievement therapy, the genuine release and healing that come with the removal of worry and the solving of financial problems. He remains linked with a fine tradition which has been a hundred years in growing, and with the thousands and thousands of fine men and women who have built up Sun Life.

THE MACAULAY CLUB

In the growth of the tradition and the development of morale in the field force the influence of the Macaulay Club can hardly be overestimated. For sixty years, since Albert Lecavalier of Montreal became first president of the club in 1911, the hope of attaining that honour has stimulated the best efforts and drawn forth the best ideas of a galaxy of brilliant men. Those who have held the office have served the company in many parts of the world. Macaulay Club presidents have been representatives of the company not only in Canada, the United States, and Great Britain, but also in Japan, Chile, Cuba, and the Philippines; while South Africa, which gave the club its presidents for eight successive years between 1959 and 1966, holds territorial honours in that respect. Of the most notable presidents, Samuel (Chummie) Hirschmann of Johannesburg and Harold M. Charlap of Philadelphia gained the honour five times and Samuel Caplan of Johannesburg four times, while Edward Lord of Tokyo, John W. Gordon of St. Catharines, Ontario, Ray H. Kotte of Cincinnati, and Victor Deitch of Indianapolis were each three times president. Supporting these leaders in promoting the growth of the company and the development of life insurance were thousands of other men who held office or gained membership in the Macaulay Club, and served year by year as an example to those who followed.

'Our staff and agency force,' said Alistair M. Campbell in 1967, 'has been drawn from men and women of varied background and education, of many races and creeds, of many languages and cultures. Yet they have melded to a common purpose in the building of a great company. They have given a loyalty that is unsurpassed in the annals of any institution. . . . The Sun Life representative is well described in the following quotation: "He invokes worthiness; he appeals to prudence, to right conduct, to human consideration, and to love. He asks men to take thought for the morrow; to make present sacrifices for future comfort – for the comfort of others. In an extravagant age, his call is to thrift."'

The man who spoke those words has piloted the company through the complex problems of an age which might, in many of its aspects, have appalled Robertson Macaulay. The present extent of the business, the huge and intricate complexity of its methods, systems, and equipment, would bewilder the earlier President. Yet all of Alistair Campbell's words in relation to the staff might well have been Macaulay's words; and by the same token the regard of the staff for the man at the head of the company remains the same. That warmth and mutual confidence, extending through all levels, has always characterized Sun Life and made the morale of the company one of its great and enduring assets. It has contributed to the success of the Macaulay Club, and it has made the achievement of membership in the Quarter Century Club one of the prized moments of a lifetime.

PRESIDENT'S MONTH

Out of the same family feeling the custom of President's Month became slowly embedded in tradition. It is now about fifty years since the idea arose among the field force of selecting one month in the year for the achievement of special production in honour of the President. Sporadic at first, and occasionally set aside because of war or troubled conditions, the custom was never abandoned and never lost its attraction. In 1945, at the close of the Second World War, President's Month was resumed in all divisions and has continued annually, with one notable addition in 1970. Following the appointment of Alistair M. Campbell as Chairman and chief executive officer, and of Anthony R. Hicks as President and chief operating officer, the month of March 1970 became Alistair Campbell Honour Month while October continued as President's Month. In each case the resulting volume of new business provided warming and tangible evidence of what the regard of the field force means.

THE HUNDRED-YEAR-OLD COMPANY

Throughout the whole year, 1970, there was renewed proof of the success and vitality of the company, of the place it has gained for itself in the modern world. That thought adds zest to the centennial. Yet beyond this the matter of perspective remains, the measuring of the scope of the achievement. As Sun Life closes the hundredth year of its history, a glance back is justified.

The assets of the company, starting with the $50,000 of capital contributed by the first shareholders in 1871, have now grown to more than $3.5 billion, all owned by the participating policyholders. Every dollar of these assets is at work somewhere in the world, contributing usefully to economic growth. At the same time, and supported by these same funds, the holders of over four million policies and group certificates enjoy life protection to a value which is now pressing on to $20 billion. Over the past century Sun Life has paid out to its policyholders $6.5 billion in benefits. Not even today's computers could calculate the number of lives that have been made more secure, the ambitions that have been realized, the wealth of human accomplishment that has been made possible by these sums. They are a part of the whole story of life insurance; and they are a great part, because Sun Life is now the twelfth largest life insurance company in the world.

SUBSIDIARIES

Sun Life remains centrally administered from its Head Office in Montreal, but the ramifications of the business are bringing certain changes. In 1969, to solve some administrative problems in connection with equity-linked policies in the United Kingdom, a wholly-owned subsidiary company was set up, Sun Life Assurance Company of Canada (U.K.) Limited. Of this company Alistair M. Campbell is Chairman and F. K. Doody, Sun Life's General Manager for Great Britain and Ireland, is Managing Director; while the Board of Directors consists of Sir George Bolton and F. K. Doody, London, and Alistair M. Campbell, Anthony R. Hicks, and Thomas M. Galt, Montreal. In the United States, as a preliminary to the introduction of variable annuity contracts, another wholly-owned subsidiary company, Sun Life Assurance Company of Canada (U.S.), was incorporated early in 1970, with its home office in Boston, Massachusetts. Alistair M. Campbell is Chairman, Anthony R. Hicks is President, and the directors are General Georges F. Doriot, Boston, Gilbert W. Humphrey, Cleveland, Ohio, and Alistair M. Campbell, Anthony R. Hicks, and Thomas M. Galt, Montreal.

OFFICES AND STAFF

Sun Life now has seventy-seven life branches in Canada, employing 1,150 sales personnel. In the United States there are sixty-seven life branches with sales personnel totalling 875; and in the whole of North America the company operates twenty-nine offices devoted to group insurance. In the United Kingdom the forty-one branches of Sun Life of Canada employ 1,025 sales representatives, while in South Africa four life branches administer the work of 180 representatives in the field. The company's mortgage loans, now totalling about $1.2 billion, are administered by eleven mortgage and real estate offices in Canada, one in the United States, and one in London, England. In addition, the company has mortgage correspondents in thirty cities in the United States. Throughout the world the total number of Sun Life personnel, including office staff and field representatives, now stands at 7,500.

With all the world-wide range of its long experience, Sun Life has continued to be a distinctively Canadian company, thoroughly aware of and responsive to the Canadian environment. Since over 90 per cent of its large international business is with English-speaking peoples, the principal working language must always be English; yet at the same time a constant effort is maintained to extend its capabilities in the other tongue. Since the early 1880s at least, Sun Life policies, rate manuals, and annual reports have been issued in French as well as in English. The value of bilingualism in Canada has always been recognized and at the present time, in Head Office alone, there are nearly five hundred completely bilingual employees. Highly skilled staffs maintain the standard of French in company literature and technical material. French-Canadian employees have advanced rapidly through the company, and have often been called to other fields in their home province where their abilities were much in demand. Four government superintendents of insurance in Quebec, a number of senior officials in the Quebec government, as well as others in French-speaking, Quebec-based insurance and financial companies, all received training with Sun Life before moving to other employment.

The company has proved itself a good corporate citizen. Public health and welfare have always been of first concern and have, in addition to medical research, been warmly and generously supported. Down through the years a company policy has developed regarding contributions, and these now reach into the hundreds of thousands of dollars annually. For a long time, through its literature, films, and work in other media, the company has done much for the cause of general education. In recent years, with the great increase in the numbers of students proceeding to universities and the increasingly onerous demands on these institutions, there has been considerable aid to higher education.

EXECUTIVE CHANGES

With Sun Life, as with all great corporations, one of the continuing problems of leadership is to provide for adequate succession. 'There is one thing I take credit for – I think I have been a good picker,' T. B. Macaulay once said, referring to the men who surrounded him; and his words were borne out by the record of three succeeding Presidents, Arthur B. Wood, George W. Bourke, and Alistair M. Campbell. Campbell himself, as the company approached the seventies, had been occupied with the same problem and was in much the same mood. While still retaining senior direction of affairs, he had provided for smooth transition and a gradual sharing of authority. The men and the arrangement decided on, with the concurrence of George Bourke and the other members of the Board of Directors, became an accomplished fact on February 10, 1970.

At the company's annual meeting on that day, Anthony Rivers Hicks and Thomas Maunsell Galt were elected directors of Sun Life. On the same day, subsequent to the annual meeting, the Board of Directors met and George W. Bourke was elected Chairman of the Executive Committee, Alistair M. Campbell, Chairman and chief executive officer, Anthony R. Hicks, President and chief operating officer, and Thomas M. Galt, Executive Vice-President.

ANTHONY RIVERS HICKS

These changes brought into the senior echelon of management two men of wide experience who had long been associated with Campbell in the inner councils of the company. Anthony Rivers Hicks, a graduate of Upper Canada College and the University of Toronto, had joined the investment department of Sun Life in 1938. Within two years the war had interrupted his career, and from 1940 to 1945 he served in the Canadian Navy, rising to the command of ships on the North Atlantic, and retiring with the rank of Lieutenant-Commander, R.C.N.(R). By 1946, as he resumed with Sun Life, he had been named Chief Clerk; by 1948 he had become supervisor of the British and Foreign Section of the investment department; and in 1956 he went to London as Resident Treasurer, British Department. Returning to Head Office in 1960, he moved rapidly through a series of appointments which further broadened his experience and increased his responsibilities. Very closely connected with the company's computer operation and with problems of administration, he became Secretary and an executive officer in 1961, Vice-President and Secretary in 1963, Vice-President, Administration in 1966, and from 1968 had been Executive Vice-President. Fifty-three years old, active and energetic, widely known and widely popular throughout the company, he came to his new office as a thoroughly seasoned, well-rounded man who had been groomed for responsibility in the best tradition of the company.

THOMAS MAUNSELL GALT

Thomas Maunsell Galt is five years younger than Hicks. A Manitoban, he had been educated at Ashbury College and had completed three years at Queen's University before entering the Royal Canadian Air Force in 1941 as an aircraftsman. After four years of service and with the rank of Flight Lieutenant, he had returned to Queen's in 1945 to take his degree. From there, with his bent as a mathematician already developed, he had gone on to the University of Manitoba, graduating in 1948 as a Bachelor of Commerce with honours in actuarial science. Later in that year he joined Sun Life as a clerk in the Mathematical Department, becoming Chief Clerk in 1950. In 1951, as he attained his Fellowship in the Society of Actuaries, he became Assistant Mathematician of Sun Life, and in 1953 he became Mathematician. By 1961 he had passed through the posts of Assistant Actuary and Associate Actuary to become Actuary and an executive officer. By 1963 he was Vice-President and Chief Actuary, and by 1968 he too had become Executive Vice-President. Now, as a director of the company and with widened responsibilities, he would have additional scope in challenging times.

THE BOARD OF DIRECTORS

All challenges, ultimately, are met by the Board of Directors. 'Throughout its history,' said Alistair Campbell in 1967, 'the Sun Life has been most fortunate in the calibre of the men it has been able to attract to join the Board of Directors. The contribution made by these gentlemen to the deliberations and decisions of a large international life insurance company like the Sun Life is tremendous. Theirs is the final responsibility and the record is of their making.' At the ninety-ninth annual meeting he had warm words for one of his departing colleagues, F. Philippe Brais, C.B.E., Q.C., LL.D., who had reached retirement age after serving on the board of the company since 1942. At the annual meetings of the two preceding years there had been similar regretful farewells for R. D. Harkness who retired in 1968 and for R. E. Stavert who retired in 1969. They had been replaced, respectively, by the election of Ian D. Sinclair of C.P.R., and Albert L. Fairley, Jr., Hollinger Mines; and the election of Hicks and Galt in 1970 completed the Board of Directors for the hundredth year.

INTO THE NEW CENTURY

As that year passes into history and the second century begins, the company looks to the future with its usual confidence. It is possible, as always, to point to problems and difficulties. In a rapidly changing economy there are new and previously unheard-of demands, and clouds lift over the horizon in forms not seen before. Yet there were few decades in the past when the same was not true. Sun Life has made its way through many economic storms, through depressions and wars, through changes in social philosophy and changes in public attitudes. It has done so, not by opposing change but by adapting itself to change, by accepting the necessity of change as a normal aspect of growth. Where it disapproves, it has said so, and sometimes rather bluntly, but of healthy innovation it has never been afraid. It has had no cause for fear because the business is soundly rooted; life insurance responds to a primary human need. The wide-spreading tree that stands as the Sun Life symbol has grown from that deep loam.

The great enterprise that was started on its way in 1871 by a few Montreal businessmen has now become the property of millions. The holders of Sun Life participating policies are the actual owners of the company. It is to them that the profits go in the form of reduced charges on a vast range of protection; and through them the ultimate motivation is provided that drives the company on. Millions of hopes are merged here, through the complex machinery of a great institution, into one simple goal: the easing of life's uncertainties by the removal of financial worry. No one knows better than the insurance man that it is only a partial answer to the problem of living, yet he has seen on many occasions how much that answer can mean. It will continue to be sought, and it will continue to respond in new and developing forms, for as long as prudent men have care for their own.

Sun Life Assurance Company of Canada, the Directors, 1970

* ALISTAIR M. CAMPBELL, F.I.A., F.S.A.
Chairman

* GEORGE W. BOURKE, F.I.A., F.S.A., LL.D., D.C.L.
Chairman of the Executive Committee

* ANTHONY R. HICKS
President

THOMAS M. GALT, F.S.A.
Executive Vice-President

* E. R. ALEXANDER
Vice-Chairman of the Board,
Gaz Métropolitain, Inc.

SIR GEORGE BOLTON, K.C.M.G.
President, Bank of London & South America Limited

FRANK M. COVERT, O.B.E., D.F.C., Q.C.
Senior Partner, Stewart, MacKeen & Covert

H. ROY CRABTREE, C.D.
Chairman and President, Wabasso Limited

ALBERT L. FAIRLEY, Jr.
President, Hollinger Mines Limited

* G. ARNOLD HART, M.B.E., LL.D., D.C.L., D.C.Sc.
Chairman and Chief Executive Officer, Bank of Montreal

LOUIS HÉBERT
Chairman and President, Banque Canadienne Nationale

G. W. HUMPHREY
Chairman of the Board, The Hanna Mining Company

* HERBERT H. LANK
Director, Du Pont of Canada Limited

* HON. HARTLAND de M. MOLSON, O.B.E.
Chairman, Molson Industries Limited

* V. W. T. SCULLY, C.M.G.
Chairman of the Board, The Steel Company of Canada, Limited

IAN D. SINCLAIR, Q.C.
President and Chief Executive Officer,
Canadian Pacific Railway Company

HON. JAMES SINCLAIR, P.C.
Deputy Chairman, Canada Cement Lafarge Ltd.

J. HERBERT SMITH, D.Sc.
Chairman of the Board, Canadian General Electric Company Limited

MARCEL VINCENT
Chairman and Chief Executive Officer, Bell Canada

* COLIN W. WEBSTER
President, Canadian Fuel Marketers Limited

* *Also member of the Executive Committee*

Officers of the Company, 1970

ALISTAIR M. CAMPBELL, F.I.A., F.S.A., *Chairman*

ANTHONY R. HICKS, *President*

THOMAS M. GALT, F.S.A., *Executive Vice-President*

W. G. ATTRIDGE
Vice-President, Agencies

G. F. S. CLARKE, F.S.A.
Vice-President and Chief Actuary

C. L. FLAVELL
Vice-President, Administration

A. R. HASLEY
Vice-President, Special Duties

A. O. MACKAY
Vice-President, Mortgages and Real Estate

W. J. MCCARTHY
Vice-President, Finance

HUGH MCLEOD, F.S.A.
Vice-President in Charge, Group

A. C. M. ROBERTSON, F.F.A.
Vice-President, Group Operations

ACTUARIAL

Associate Actuaries:

S. M. T. BAILEY, F.I.A., F.S.A.
T. S. BELL, F.S.A.
J. J. P. DUKACZ, F.S.A.
J. R. GARDNER, F.S.A.
A. H. GRAY, F.S.A.
D. G. LEYBOURNE, F.S.A.
FRANCOIS VACHON, F.S.A.

Product Co-ordination Officer:

J. G. TYRRELL, C.L.U.

GEORGE W. BOURKE, F.I.A., F.S.A., *Chairman of the Executive Committee*

A. G. DENNIS
Executive Officer, Agencies

S. J. GOWDY
Executive Officer, Personnel

J. H. HARRISON
Treasurer

P. R. MACGIBBON
Secretary

A. G. MCCRACKEN
General Counsel

J. W. PARKINSON, C.G.A.
Comptroller

G. W. WILSON, F.S.A.
Actuary and
Executive Officer, Underwriting

D. H. WOODHOUSE, M.D.
Medical Director

Assistant Superintendent,
Mathematical Services:
R. ALLAN

Assistant Superintendents,
Pension Trust:
W. C. FAIRLEY
D. RUTGERS, ASSOC. C.L.U.

ADMINISTRATION

Senior Planning Officer:
JACQUES DESCHÊNES, F.S.A.

Planning Officer:
H. R. BENTLEY, F.L.M.I.

Associate Planning Officers:
N. B. CALVIN
M. N. LARSEN

Assistant Planning Officers:
C. E. CARTMEL, F.L.M.I.
R. A. CURRY, C.A.
R. J. EMERY, F.L.M.I.
C. D. GORE
T. L. HOOD
G. E. MITCHELL
S. F. TRASK, C.G.A., F.L.M.I.

General Superintendent, Policy Administration:
J. T. BRADBURY, F.L.M.I.

Superintendent, Policy Administration:
R. K. L. WELBOURN, C.G.A., F.L.M.I.

Assistant Superintendents, Policy Administration:
J. E. COLLEY
H. E. MOORE, F.L.M.I.

Assistant Actuary:
C. L. F. WATCHORN, F.S.A.

AGENCY

General Superintendents of Agencies:
F. H. FRIZZELL
D. E. HART, C.L.U.
G. P. PIM

Superintendents of Agencies:
D. S. A. BELL
O. A. DARILEK
GUY DE PUYJALON
C. C. DOVEY, C.L.U.
G. J. FERGUSON
J. R. HANNAM
C. J. D. LEAMY
M. D. LOUCKS
W. H. REYNOLDS
C. M. ROOT
K. M. STEWART

COMPTROLLER'S

Internal Auditor:
R. F. HAWKES, C.A.

Assistant Comptrollers:
G. A. DAVIES, C.G.A.
W. H. P. MCGOWAN, C.A.

GROUP

General Superintendent, Group Sales and Service:
H. R. FACEY

Superintendents:
Group Sales and Service:
W. R. PEARO

Group Pensions:
W. F. WATSON

Associate Group Actuaries:
F. G. MOREWOOD, F.S.A.
O. A. REED, F.S.A.
LOUIS ROBERT, F.S.A.

Superintendent, Group Administration:
A. D. LANG

Superintendent, Administration:
J. E. BINGHAM

Administrative Services Officer:
L. M. CLARK

Associate Superintendents of Agencies:
B. R. DAVIS
J. LECHEMINANT

Assistant Superintendents of Agencies:
A. A. BOYCE
C. L. JEFFREY, C.L.U.
G. A. JEUTTER
D. F. MANN
C. P. O'BRIEN
J. PALARDY
R. M. PEACOCK
P. F. RAMAGE
J. T. STAFFORD
K. A. M. WALKER

Taxation Officer:
F. W. BAKER

Associate Superintendent, Group Pensions:
J. S. GUNN

Assistant Group Actuaries:
J. GREGOIRE, F.S.A.
A. PARODOS, F.S.A.

Assistant Superintendents, Group Sales and Service:
D. A. SMITH
C. W. STITT

Assistant Personnel Officer, Group:
W. S. BRISBANE

Assistant Superintendents, Group Administration:
L. G. CLARKSON, C.G.A., F.L.M.I.
G. M. GRASSBY, A.S.A.

INVESTMENT

Associate Treasurers:

D. I. ABRAMS
G. N. CAUGHLIN, C.F.A., F.L.M.I.
H. B. FEWKES, C.F.A.
J. C. GORDON, C.F.A.
J. S. LANE, C.F.A.
J. E. R. LOCKHART
R. R. NAUDIE, C.F.A.
G. POLISZCZUK

Senior Economist:

J. W. POPKIN

Assistant Economist:

J. R. SCOTT-RAM

Assistant Treasurers:

J. H. BAIRD
J. M. CASTONGUAY
J. FRIZZELL
J. M. GREANEY
E. A. M. HAYHURST, C.G.A.
C. A. LEMIRE
J. G. LYNCH-STAUNTON
K. MCDONALD, C.F.A.
L. M. MURPHY
M. P. PRESCOTT
G. D. SMITH, C.F.A.
A. G. F. WIRTH
W. D. YEATES, C.A.

LEGAL

Associate General Counsel:

J. A. BRABANT
W. J. HULBIG
LUC PLAMONDON
B. R. RITCHIE, Q.C.

Assistant General Counsel:

D. D. HORN
ROBERTA K. SHAPIRO

MEDICAL

Associate Medical Directors:

F. A. D'ABADIE, M.D.
T. R. HALE, M.D.
J. G. HELLSTROM, M.D.

PERSONNEL

Personnel Officer:

W. W. MCALPINE

Assistant Personnel Officers:

W. F. BADKE, F.L.M.I.
R. F. JOHNSON
W. B. SIEBRASSE
FRANCES L. WRIGHT

SECRETARIAL

Associate Secretary:

G. E. MERRITT

Assistant Secretary:

D. FORD

Superintendents of Claims:

C. L. BRODIE
K. JOHNSTON

SPECIAL DUTIES

Public Relations Officer:

J. A. NORMAN, CPRS ACC.

Assistant Public Relations Officer:

PIERRE BOILEAU, CPRS ACC.

Superintendent of Mortgages:
G. A. GOLDEN, M.A.I.

Associate Superintendents of Mortgages and Real Estate:
C. R. CUMMINS, M.A.I.
J. S. HARVEY
F. L. STARK

U.S. Mortgage and Real Estate Officer:
G. L. CAMPBELL

Assistant Superintendents of Mortgages and Real Estate:
J. D. BURWELL
M. A. CANNING
T. A. J. MOLL

Superintendent of Real Estate Investments:
W. D. THOMAS

Assistant Superintendent of Real Estate Investments:
R. J. W. WRIGHT

Assistant Counsel:
B. S. TAYLOR

Associate Superintendents of Claims:
C. H. HOPKINS
F. G. OGILVIE

Assistant Superintendents of Claims:
W. T. FAGG
J. FRASER
J. N. MANNERS

UNDERWRITING

Underwriting Officer:
D. L. GAUER, F.S.A.

Underwriting Research Officer:
T. M. LAWRENCE

BRITISH DEPARTMENT

General Manager for Great Britain and Ireland:
F. K. DOODY

Manager of Agencies:
J. A. BRINDLE

SOUTH AFRICA

Manager for South Africa:
P. S. MATHEWSON

Resident Treasurer for Southern Africa:
C. R. GLEDHILL

Assistant Underwriting Officers:
R. W. BUCKLAND
J. J. MACKNIGHT, F.L.M.I.

Resident Secretary:
J. C. CLELAND
Resident Treasurer:
P. W. DYSON
Resident Actuary:
M. C. POLMAN, F.I.A.

Consulting Medical Officer:
S. ORAM, M.D.

Incorporators of the Company, and Directors Who Have Served since Organization

George Stephen	Incorporator, 1865
Mathew Hamilton Gault	"
Thomas Gordon	"
William Dow	"
James Glennon	"
George H. Frothingham	"
Alexander Walker Ogilvie	"
Henry Thomas	"
James Hutton	"
Henry Mulholland	"
James Ferrier, the younger	"
George Stephen	Provisional Director, 1865
Amable Prévost	"
John Caverhill	"
Benjamin Lyman	"
Theodore Doucet	"
Thomas Tiffin	"
William Darling	"
George Winks	"
George Stephen	Provisional Director, May 1870
George Winks	"
Thomas Gordon	"
Henry Mulholland	"
George H. Frothingham	"
Alexander Walker Ogilvie	"
Andrew Frederick Gault	"
James Hutton	"
Mathew Hamilton Gault	"
Thomas Workman, M.P.	Provisional Director, October 1870
Henry Mulholland	"
Andrew Frederick Gault	"
James Hutton	"
Alexander Walker Ogilvie	"
Alex. Buntin	"
John Rankin	"
T. James Claxton	"
Charles Alexander	"
Mathew Hamilton Gault	"
§ Mathew Hamilton Gault	Director 1871-1884
§ Thomas Workman	1871-1889
Andrew Frederick Gault	1871-1887
Henry Mulholland	1871-1878
Charles Alexander	1871-1879

	T. James Claxton	Director	1871-1883
	Charles J. Coursol		1871-1874
§	James Hutton		1871-1882
	John Rankin		1871-1875
	Alex. Buntin		1871-1873
§	Hon. Alexander Walker Ogilvie		1873-1902
	Hugh McLennan		1876-1877
§	T. M. Bryson		1877-1883
	John McLennan		1878-1880
	David Morrice		1879-1885
	Edmond J. Barbeau		1880-1885
	Hon. John Boyd		1882-1884
	Charles Cassils		1883-1883
§‡	Samuel H. Ewing		1883-1923
§†‡	Robertson Macaulay		1883-1915
§	William J. Withall		1884-1898
	J. S. McLachlan		1884-1886
	Robert Anderson		1885-1896
§	Alex. Macpherson		1885-1904
§	Murdoch McKenzie		1887-1904
§	James Tasker		1887-1910
§	J. P. Cleghorn		1890-1911
§†‡	Thomas Bassett Macaulay		1896-1942
§‡	J. R. Dougall		1898-1934
§†	Abner Kingman		1902-1930
§	Charles Cushing		1904-1910
§†	John McKergow		1905-1920
‡	William Massey Birks		1911-1950
†‡	Hon. Raoul Dandurand		1911-1942
	H. Warren K. Hale		1911-1918
§†	Sir Herbert S. Holt		1911-1941
‡	Charles R. Hosmer		1911-1927
	George E. Drummond		1912-1919
	Dr. Herbert R. Macaulay		1915-1923
†	John W. Ross		1918-1946
‡	Robert Adair		1919-1937
‡	Carl Riordon		1920-1958
†*	Arthur B. Wood		1923-1952
†	Hon. Lorne C. Webster		1923-1941
‡	Hon. James C. Tory		1926-1934
†	C. E. Neill		1926-1931
†	J. W. McConnell		1926-1938
‡	Hon. L. A. Taschereau		1928-1952
†*	Ross H. McMaster		1928-1962

†	C. B. McNaught	Director	1928-1934
†	E. W. Beatty		1930-1943
†	Rt. Hon. Arthur B. Purvis		1933-1941
†*	E. A. Macnutt		1934-1955
†	Morris W. Wilson		1937-1946
	John A. Tory		1938-1950
†*	Hon. Charles A. Dunning		1941-1958
†	G. W. Spinney		1942-1948
†*	Harold Crabtree		1942-1956
	Hon. F. Philippe Brais		1942-1970
	Arthur Cross		1942-1966
†	W. M. Neal		1944-1948
†*	George W. Bourke		1946-
†*	Frederick Johnson		1946-1966
*	Ross Clarkson		1948-1966
	R. E. Stavert		1948-1969
	J. S. D. Tory		1950-1965
	A. E. Grauer		1950-1961
	Gordon R. Ball		1952-1959
	George Gund		1952-1966
	James McG. Stewart		1952-1955
*	John A. Fuller		1954-1970
*	R. D. Harkness		1954-1968
	Albert S. Fraser		1955-1966
*	Hon. H. de M. Molson		1955-
*	Alistair M. Campbell		1956-
	Sir George Bolton		1957-
*	E. R. Alexander		1958-
*	V. W. T. Scully		1958-
*	G. Arnold Hart		1959-
	H. Roy Crabtree		1960-
	M. M. Walter		1960-1960
*	Colin W. Webster		1961-
	Hon. James Sinclair		1962-
	Louis Hébert		1963-
	Frank M. Covert		1966-
	R. A. Emerson		1966-1966
	G. W. Humphrey		1966-
	J. Herbert Smith		1966-
	Marcel Vincent		1966-

* Herbert H. Lank	Director	1966-
Ian D. Sinclair		1968-
Albert L. Fairley, Jr.		1969-
* Anthony R. Hicks		1970-
Thomas M. Galt		1970-

* *Member, Executive Committee*	*(since 1951)*
† *Member, Investment Committee*	*(1915-1951)*
‡ *Member, General Committee*	*(1915-1951)*
§ *Member, Finance or Investment Committee*	*(prior to 1915)*

Presidents of the Company in Its First Hundred Years

1. THOMAS WORKMAN (1813-1889)
   President, 1871-1889

2. ROBERTSON MACAULAY (1833-1915)
   President and Managing Director, 1889-1908
   President, 1908-1915

3. THOMAS BASSETT MACAULAY (1860-1942)
   President and Managing Director, 1915-1932
   President, 1932-1934
   Chairman of the Board, 1934-1935
   Chairman Emeritus, 1935-1942

4. ARTHUR BARTON WOOD (1870-1952)
   President and Managing Director, 1934-1946
   President, 1946-1950
   Chairman of the Board, 1950-1952

5. GEORGE WESLEY BOURKE (1896-)
   President, 1950-1962
   Chairman of the Board, 1962-1970
   Chairman of the Executive Committee, 1970-

6. ALISTAIR MATHESON CAMPBELL (1905-)
   President, 1962-1970
   Chairman, 1970-

7. ANTHONY RIVERS HICKS (1916-)
   President, 1970-

Members of the 1970 Managers' Consultation Committees

CANADIAN DIVISIONS

I. F. DeWest, Chairman	Vancouver Arbutus
W. J. Campbell	Thunder Bay
J. P. Chauvin, C.L.U.	Montreal Cartier
H. K. Daues	Toronto Yonge
J. J. Driscoll, C.L.U.	Winnipeg Red River
J. T. Gray, C.L.U.	Toronto Scarborough
F. Therrien, C.L.U.	Rimouski

UNITED STATES DIVISIONS

H. A. Dahl, Chairman	Atlanta
G. J. Ackel	New Orleans
R. W. Buchanan	Newark Essex
E. E. Codere	Chicago
J. T. Diskin	Detroit Northland
R. D. Ekblad	Houston
G. B. Gonzalez	San Juan

GROUP DIVISION

E. S. Stuart, Chairman	Toronto Group
A. G. S. Arnot	Montreal Group
J. A. Boland	British Columbia Group
H. H. Earl	Philadelphia Group
G. E. Sutherland	Eastern Canada Group
J. H. Watkins	Chicago Group

BRITISH DIVISION (*Managers' Consultative Committee*)

J. A. Brindle, Chairman	Manager of Agencies
M. R. M. Alexander	Nottingham
F. D. Foden	Colchester
E. J. Lloyd	Plymouth
K. W. Odgers	London Westminster
F. Smith	London Langham
J. B. Smith	Reading
E. W. Sparrow	Southampton

Macaulay Club Officers – Membership Year 1970-1971

PRESIDENT

Heitner, Solomon, C.L.U.	Baltimore

CANADIAN DIVISIONS

SENIOR VICE-PRESIDENT

Bourbeau, Jacques	Montreal Cartier

VICE-PRESIDENTS

Eyford, D. D., C.L.U.	Edmonton Jasper
Abbott, William A., C.L.U.	Vancouver Arbutus
Tainsh, W. B.	Edmonton Jasper
Carrara, Aldo	Montreal St. James
Dick, Donald A., C.L.U.	Winnipeg Red River
Carrier, Robert	Quebec Champlain
Herberman, Ben, C.L.U.	Toronto Eglinton
Russel, James B., C.L.U.	Toronto Tower
Singh, Sabu	Vancouver Central
Weinstein, S. L.	Edmonton Empire
Seifeddine, Sami	Montreal Mansfield
Côté, Andre	Montreal Lafontaine
Ross, Walter Hugh, C.L.U.	Edmonton Jasper
Sayer, Selim	Montreal Queen Mary
MacDonald, F. R. C.	Halifax
Ouellette, Larry P., C.L.U.	Windsor
Bryan, John C., C.L.U.	Hamilton Central
Bayne, Allan P.	Winnipeg Red River
Artzy, Mrs. Dvorah	Montreal Cavendish
Marchbank, V. H.	Winnipeg Red River

UNITED STATES DIVISIONS

SENIOR VICE-PRESIDENT

Hakemian, Sam C.	Detroit Northland

VICE-PRESIDENTS

Katz, Lawrence G., C.L.U.	Houston
Themelis, George H.	Boston Beacon
Miller, Marc	Philadelphia Chestnut
Fraga, Antonio D.	San Juan
Batdorf, John W.	Philadelphia Chestnut
Ross, Norman S., C.L.U.	Houston
Anderson, Mark E.	Salt Lake City
Hatton, Robert J.	San Juan
Casten, Jay E.	Spokane
Flanigan, Mrs. Helen H.	St. Louis
Bollato, John A., C.L.U.	Houston
Platt, Kenneth J.	Newark Essex
Orner, Hal G.	New Orleans

Greiss, Stanley M., C.L.U.	Houston
Donohoe, Thomas H.	Jacksonville
Berk, Kurt	Houston
Feinberg, Morris	Atlanta
Manalo, P. D.	Philippines

SOUTH AFRICA DIVISION

SENIOR VICE-PRESIDENT

Cost, Byron	Johannesburg City

VICE-PRESIDENTS

Abed, G.	Cape Town
Thomas, M.	Cape Town
Patel, Essop	Johannesburg City
Louis, Myer	Johannesburg Central
Moodley, S. A.	Durban
Ramsamy, Joe	Johannesburg City
Tagari, Hoosein	Johannesburg City

BRITISH DIVISION

FIRST VICE-PRESIDENT

Senior, E. L.	Leeds

VICE-PRESIDENTS

Churchman, A. E.	London Chancery Lane
Hager, B. W.	London Mayfair
Vann, D. R.	Birmingham Warwick
Morley, B. G. W.	London Langham
Whitrow, H. T.	Reading
Clarke, C. G.	Liverpool
Peek, D. J.	Bromley
Reynders, D. C.	London Trafalgar
Abbott, H. S.	London Haymarket

Index of Names, Institutions, etc., Mentioned in the Text